DATE DUE

D0934310

COMMUNISM IN CHINA

AS REPORTED FROM HANKOW IN 1932

COMMUNISM IN CHINA

AS REPORTED FROM HANKOW
IN 1932
BY O. EDMUND CLUBB

NEW YORK & LONDON 1968

COLUMBIA UNIVERSITY PRESS

PREFACE

SINCE the overthrow of the Nationalist regime in 1949 and the establishment of a Communist government in Peking, many researchers have worked to discover the causes of the Communist victory over the Nationalists and to unravel the mysteries of the Communist leadership's policies. Earlier, much less effort was devoted to the study of the Chinese revolutionary process. This was true for American governmental services even as for individual scholars. Dr. Dorothy Borg, who made an intensive study of relevant State Department documents, in her 1964 book, *The United States and the Far Eastern Crisis of 1933-1938,* devoted a chapter to discussing "Views of American Officials on the Chinese Communists and the Sian Incident." She took due note of the work of a vice consul at Hankow, who in 1932 had prepared a long report on Chinese Communism, and "from 1932 to the time of the Kuomintang-Communist rapprochement of September 1937...appears to have been alone in his efforts to supply the State Department with first-hand material (official documents et cetera) on the Chinese Communists and to provide some consistent analysis of their activities." I was that young vice consul; the present text is my report of 1932.

I had gone to China to be a language attaché at the American Legation in Peiping (Peking) early in 1929, a few months after the establishment of the National Government at Nanking. In that year there had been two major civil wars among the victorious Nationalists; in 1930 the biggest of the Nationalist wars was fought, resulting in the establishment of a dissident regime in Peiping, which lasted only a short time. The country was in disorder. Interminable civil wars, political disorganization, economic chaos, and natural disasters had brought deep misery to tens of millions of the long-suffering *lao-pai-hsing* (the Old Hundred Names, the common people).

On April 29, 1931, when I finished my Chinese-language course at Peiping, I submitted a 36-page voluntary report to the Legation under the title "Disruptive Elements in China." In the introductory paragraph, I wrote: "It has never been truer than in China that, where one part of the social structure is weakened, the whole is rendered liable to collapse." I sketched the history of the turbulent period, beginning in 1919, when Chinese were invited to attend the First Comintern Congress at Moscow, down to 1931. Recording the organization of the Chinese Communist Party in 1921, I treated briefly the 1924-1927 collaboration between the Communists and the revolutionary Kuomintang, under the overall guidance of Soviet adviser Michael Borodin. Springboarding from the 1927 break between the two parties, I addressed myself more particularly to the major question of the revolutionary potential of China. Against the background of the divisions between Chiang Kai-shek and other Kuomintang militarists I discussed the composition of the Communist leadership and recounted various reports of recent military actions under that leadership. I laid down a general proposition:

While political revolutions may be brought about by reason of intellectual dissatisfaction, personal ambition, or some other of the various cultural motives that actuate the daily life of society, social revolution (that is, a definite turning over of the whole social structure) has but two causes, working in conjunction. These causes are mass dissatisfaction, and ideas of social change comprehended by those masses (even though in the barest outline or by slogan). One factor without the other does not operate, but given the two a revolutionary situation ripens, ready to be organized and led—somewhere. The final destination may be discovered to be as bad as or worse than the starting point, but a beginning revolutionary movement never has a worse situation as objective, so that the logic that is evident in the evolved factual situation does not apply to stop its prior development.

I dwelt in detail on the current condition of the Chinese people by reason of misgovernment, the usurious relations between landlord and tenant, unbridled commodity speculation, and the impact of industrialization. I remarked the existence at that time of some 20 to 25 million famine sufferers in the northern and northwestern provinces and observed that "It can fairly definitely be stated that the present conditions in China are such as have in the past led to rebellion of the population." I said that "the discontent which finds expression in such movements as peasant revolt needs but a revolutionary ideaology [*sic*] to become a real social revolution." Upon such a culture as that discovered in China, bare of political superstructure, "there may be erected with equal facility Wang An-shih's state socialism of the Sung Dynasty or communism in the 20th century." I ended my initial essay on "Disruptive Elements in China" with the comment:

"No other conclusion seems necessary than that the social revolution that had its conception in the impact of the Western industrial revolution with China in the latter quarter of the 19th century, and its birth in 1919, has not yet completed its period of development."

When in mid-1931 I took up my assignment as vice consul at Hankow, flood waters were nearing the top of the dikes holding the deep Yangtze. The raging waters shortly overflowed the riverbanks to add to the seemingly endless suffering of the afflicted people. It was at this time that the second "bandit-suppression campaign" ended, unsuccessfully. It was directed by the Nationalist regime at the "Red Bandits" then roaming the countryside, some of them in the immediate vicinity of Wuhan (as the three neighboring towns Wuchang, Hanyang, and Hankow were called), which so short a time before had been the capital of the revolutionary Kuomintang. The term "Red Bandits" was the Nanking regime's pejorative term for tens of thousands of desperate men engaged in rebellion against Nationalist authority under Communist, or presumed Communist, leadership.

The line of demarcation among troops in revolt, professional bandits, peasants driven to banditry by desperation, and revolutionaries was sometimes exceedingly fine. I focused my attention on the revolutionaries. Projecting my work of 1931, I continued to study the turbulent social phenomenon of which I was now so close a witness. It was at the end of my first year at Hankow that I wrote my report, "Communism in China," to picture the internal, organizational aspects of the revolutionary movement and to assess its importance. The report was based on Chinese-language and English-language newspaper items, information obtained from the few Communist publications I could lay my hands on, miscellaneous reports, and some direct testimony given by missionaries and others.

My covering memorandum set forth some definitions and established a background frame of reference for the report, but it was also suggestive of the difficulties I encountered in writing my essay, given the time, place, and circumstances. The Nationalists had outlawed the Communists and were engaged in a major effort to hunt them down and annihilate them, whether in battle or by individual execution. Objective informationn regarding those outlaws was not easy to come by. I documented my report as well as I could, but this was a virgin field of investigaton, and the possiblity of cross-checking information was exceedingly limited in a town without even a public library. I do not claim that my work of 1932 was without error. I included a report of the death of Chou En-lai, but that person is still very much alive today, as are various other Communist leaders, including Mao Tse-tung himself, who were reported by the Nationalists to have been killed several times over through the years of strife. I forecast the probable early departure of Chiang Kai-shek from the political scene (he had made a comeback from his second retirement from office only the preceding spring), but it was actually seventeen more years before he lost power in China to the "Red Bandits" he had both collaborated with and fought against; and he still exercises dictatorial power on Formosa. I used a faulty Chinese character for one Communist leader, writing his name Chang Kuo-shou instead of Chang Kuo-tao; and I was unable to discover Chinese characters for some Communist proper names today well known (at least to scholars). But my report was in all senses of the word a pioneering effort, and it was as such that I offered it—and as such that it stands up, I believe, even today. I therefore permit that essay to speak for itself, except for quoting the ending, incorporating my forecast of over thirty-five years ago:

The development [in China] will apparently be slowly toward a form of State socialism, with the San Min Chu I and the Kuomintang and its ghostly adviser all to be dropped. It is to be expected that the actual pressure of economic circumstance will make requisite an attitude on the part of the new Chinese nation that will not be characterized generally by open hostility toward other countries. But that may not be said certainly.

The issue posed in the final two sentences of the quotation remains open, to be determined by the future.

O. EDMUND CLUBB

June 9, 1968

MEMORANDUM

There is submitted herewith, as of possible
interest, a study on the subject of Communism in
China; it is meant to be the logical development of
the writer's essay "Disruptive Elements in China",
dated April 29, 1931, and would properly be coordi-
nated with it. As before, because of defective
research facilities the plausible has often had to
be accepted as true, even though the margin of
certainty might have been small. The most reliance
for material has been upon the PEKING & TIENTSIN TIMES
and the TA KUNG PAO, adjudged to be respectively the
best English - and Chinese-launguage newspapers in
China; where the question was one of Communist policy,
Communist material was used so far as available (but
the Chinese libraries, both public and private, keep
no records of the Chinese revolution except such as
are approved by current orthodox opinion).

The term "Communist" is used to signify a member
of the Communist Party; the word "Red", as employed in
the text, is used as the revolutionaries apply it to
themselves, designating a participant in the revolutionary
agrarian movement that is developing in central China under
the direction of the Communist Party - and he may or may
not be a member-Communist. There is no regard given to
the degree of understanding that the rank and file of
the rebels have for the doctrines they profess. It is
evident that the select group of leaders of a revolution
commonly have the knowledge of the direction they wish to
go, but that a few slogans suffice for the great majority
of the persons following them; this is true of most mass
movements. Again, the terminology ordinarily accepted
as having a revolutionary signification has not been
employed here as inclusive of banditry, which is,
oppositely, discussed only incidentally to the main
subject. The attempt has been to present an integrated
picture of one section of the Chinese scene with the
general theme as true as possible to the facts adduced.
The material mostly dates only up to April 20, 1932.

                    O. Edmund Clubb.

Hankow, China, April 30, 1932.

COMMUNISM IN CHINA

Table of Contents

LIST OF ABBREVIATIONS USED

ACLF   -   All-China Labor Federation

CC   -   Central Committee (of the
                         Communist Party)

CCP   -   Chinese Communist Party

CEC   -   Central Executive Committee

COMINTERN   -   (Third) Communist International

CP   -   Communist Party

PGCSR   -   Provisional Government of the
                         Chinese Soviet Republic

POLITBUREAU   -   Central Political Bureau

PROFINTERN   -   (Red) Trade-Union International

MOPR   -   International Organization for
                         Revolutionary Aid

YCL   -   Young Communists League

THE CHINESE REVOLUTION

"The pleasing fiction that a new China
naturally friendly to the U. S. is
destined to emerge is just as likely
to prove absurd as the similar delusion
about the new Russia." Frank H. Simonds.

I. INTRODUCTION

In a series of three articles, Dr. Hu Shih
in 1930 pointed out that, although knowledge is
difficult even as Sun Yat-sen had conceived it to
be (知難行易), action, in the sense of
execution of known policies, has in it many
elements of difficulty. He enlarged upon his
thesis with a pungent criticism of the Kuomintang
idea of "the period of tutelage", contending that
the only training for democracy is practice at
democracy, and particularly questioning the ability
of the Kuomintang rulers to lead the people in
democratic political practices inasmuch as they
themselves had no knowledge of what they professed
to teach. Dr. Hu Shih became the Kuomintang's
pet bete noire of the moment, receiving a harsh
reprimand from the party for his heresy, and the
Ministry of Education ordered him to desist from
further criticism of the San Min Chu I and other
doctrines of Sunyatsenism. He soared in the popular
esteem of the student group, and that was all.

The rule of the Kuomintang in its pure state,
unadulterated by Leftist doctrine, has lasted from
1927 until the present - five years - and all the
concrete results of its activities indicate that

Hu Shih's strictures were nicely pertinent. The
grasping militarism that has been the inseparable
companion of the Kuomintang regime has given the
people neither anything of political democracy,
nor any of the economic betterment which sometimes
partially justifies strict dictatorship, or tyranny.
The fanfaronade of the militarists' mouthpieces has
not served to conceal the fact that the country and
its people are becoming progressively poorer despite
the grandiose programs for economic progress that
appear perennially in the Chinese political scene.
As Dr. Hu Shih held, "To know is difficult, but to
act is difficult too" - and this aphorism is
especially valid when greed for wealth and power
prevents the implementation of what poor truths have
been arrived at.

According to orthodox revolutionary theory,
before there can be a socialistic proletarian
revolution in a feudalistic country there will
ordinarily occur first a nationalistic "bourgeois
revolution". As regards China, Trotsky considered
that a popular conference should be held, whereupon
the proletariat should grasp the leadership and call
upon the people of the country to rise and seize the
reins of power as in Russia's October Revolution.
Stalin thought differently, and following the Stalin
line of thought was of course his representative, the
seasoned revolutionary Borodin, who supported firmly
the policy of cooperation between the Communist and

Nationalist Parties, as originally agreed upon
between him and Sun Yat-sen. Trotsky in his
polemics against the power of Stalin accused the
latter of committing the Comintern to a policy of
discouraging the agrarian revolution in China as
early as October 1926, in order not to embarrass
the Kuomintang at its work of nationalistic
revolution. That such was substantially Stalin's
policy is seen in a review of the policies of
Borodin; moreover, Document No. 3 of the papers
seized in the raid on the Soviet Embassy in Peking
on April 6, 1927, purporting to be an instruction
(date not given) to the Military Attaché regarding
policy to be followed in China, directed that

> "Every attention must be paid at present to
> lend to the revolutionary movement in China
> an EXCLUSIVELY national character. To this
> end it is necessary to carry on agitation in
> favor of the Kuomintang as of the party of
> the national independence of China..... Be
> careful not to carry out at present the
> communistic program. This might strengthen
> Chang Tso-lin's position and augment the
> split in the Kuomintang. We have categorically
> ordered Borodin to abstain for the present from
> too strong pressure on the capitalistic elements,
> having in mind the aim to keep in the Kuomintang
> all classes of the population, including the
> bourgeoisie, until the fall of Chang Tso-lin."

Also in accord with that general orientation was the
policy expressed in the Manifesto of the Central
Executive Committee of the Kuangtung Section of the
Chinese Communist Party (CCP) on April 1, 1926:

> "The Nationalist Government is recognized by the
> Communist Party as the basis for nationalist
> revolution and as the headquarters of anti-
> imperialism in China. Therefore we have gathered

the workers and peasants to do their best to
help the Nationalist Government in its
consolidation and development.   ......we
must unite in a common struggle for the
common object of overthrowing imperialism
and militarism and establishing a United
Nationalist Government of all China."
NATION, 122:636

The desire of the Communist International
(Comintern) was to exercise a directive function in
the wave of revolutionary nationalism that was
sweeping the country, the while it would be enabled
to carry on activities of organization and propaganda
looking toward the swinging of the nationalistic
revolution into a more advanced socialistic stage.
Borodin and the other Soviet advisers supplied the
comparatively radical Cantonese followers of Sun
Yat-sen with both the technical knowledge and material
sinews of revolt, giving a purpose and momentum to the
movement that sufficed to carry it on to Peking even
though the peak of its strength had been reached at
the Yangtze River. The "cleansing" that followed on
the heels of the splitting apart of the CCP and the
Kuomintang swept out of the group in political control
all elements of Leftist liberalism as well as Leftist
radicalism, the residual philosophy being the same as
prevailed under Yuan Shih-k'ai (袁世凱) and Tuan
C'hi-jui (段祺瑞). Although the force of its
initial drive carried the Kuomintang Army to Peking,
there was little left of the original movement besides
the militaristic elements that were bent on feudal
spoilation and were bound to bicker over those spoils.

The history of China since 1927 has been one of the
progressive disillusionment of sometime supporters
of the Kuomintang, and their banishment into the
Party's Opposition - "The Reactionaries" - where
they gradually coalesce into new groups.

It has very often been true in the history of
nations that efforts at suppression, whether from
within or outside the State, have proved in the end
to be of considerable assistance to revolutionary
movements, the pressure integrating the separate
elements into a strong unity and giving it shape. In
the case of China, what might have been the long-
overdue liberal revolution, leading to the establishment of a mildly socialistic democratic State was cut
short soon after its birth, and its essential parts
were expelled and dissipated. The few phrases of
liberal democracy the dynasts continued to give lip-
service to - having none of their own - have become
empty and meaningless, for the actions of the ruling
group are an oppressive contradiction of the doctrine.
There is no congruence between the two. In such a
combination of circumstances the Chinese Left movement,
which might have been leavened with the sober judgment
of the intelligentsia had it been promised the
possibility of liberal political and economic reform
within the framework of the existing system of
government, has been forced, by the vicious hardships
suffered in its position as outlaw, into a bitter
rebellion which is sweeping the oppressed - liberal

students and all - with a savage hatred of the
existing regime in China. Fearless, almost fanatic,
conviction in their doctrinairism has become a
characteristic of the leaders of the revolt of the
Chinese masses. Where the course of things might
have resulted in the slower natural growth of
liberalism, the great masses of the people have
been driven prematurely to extreme radical measures.
The Chinese Communist Party is now the chief
revolutionary organization in China, and its
beginning as a separate entity may be dated from
July 13, 1927, when it broke off from the Kuomintang.

II. ARMED REVOLT

1. Post-1927 Period (1927-1930).

Following the institution of counter-revolutionary
measures by Chiang Kai-shih (蔣介石) in Shanghai
and Canton after March 1927, and particularly after
the Chengchow Conference with Feng Yü-hsiang (馮玉祥),
the Communist leaders discovered that they had come to
a parting of the ways before they had anticipated. The
order came from Moscow to form a Communist Army of
70,000 troops without delay to meet the emergency, but
this could not be accomplished. The CCP, starting out
with some 40 members at the time of its entrance into
the Kuomintang in 1924, had not yet become strong
enough to lead any large section of the population
against the still popular Kuomintang. There would have
to be first the bankruptcy of the Kuomintang and the
crystallization of the disparate groups that were
exorcized by it as heterodox.

Such small military support as the Left possessed immediately after the fall of the Hankow Government was the troops of Chang Fa-k'uei's (張 發 奎) Ironsides commanded by Ho Lung (賀 龍) and Yeh T'ing (葉 挺); they took Nanchang on August 1, 1927, but were driven out after six days by troops under the leadership of Chang Fa-kuei himself. Li Li-san (李 立 三) had been appointed Chairman of the ephemeral Soviet Government. On September 25th of that year the same army, now led by Yeh T'ing, captured Swatow; an attempt was made to set up a Soviet Government there also, but the regime fell on October 1st. The Left movement that developed in Canton with the taking of the city by Chang Fa-k'uei from Li Chi-shen's (李 濟 琛) troops, with the assistance of the radical Canton labor unions, and apparently for the benefit of the waning Wang Ching-wei (汪 精 衛), culminated in the Red uprising of December 11, 1927. The insurrection of the "Peasants', Workers' and Soldiers' Army", in which evidently participated Ho Lung, Yeh T'ing, and Chu Teh (朱 德), continued through three days of fighting accompanied by looting, burning, and bloody killing. It was suppressed with a ferocity that was bloodier still. It is stated that 700 "enemies of the people" were killed by the rebels, and that the Government forces in the period immediately following the putting-down of the revolt killed 6,000. The trek of the dispossessed Left-Wing elements homeward to Canton, "The Cradle of the Chinese Revolution", seemed to have resulted in their complete obliteration. On December 14th the Nanking Government informed the U. S. S. R. that relations between the two countries were broken off, and there was again the appearance of a China troubled by no more than civil war, and banditry.

Underneath the surface, however, the struggle continued violently for several months. The rebels on the one hand, with their three nearly successful coups, still felt that it was possible to seize control in the name of the proletariat; those in power, with the lessons of Nanchang, Swatow, and Canton, before them, also visualized the possibility of such a contingency, and took strict precautions looking toward the complete extermination of all elements that were suspected of being tarred with the Red brush. In Hankow, there was unearthed a Communist plot for another bid for power in the month of January 1928, and strict martial law was enforced for several weeks after January 17th; there were reported executions of 112 "Communists" in that city for the period from December 17th to January 31, 1928, and a total of 200 executions for the two succeeding months. Similar conditions existed in the other chief cities of the southern half of China.

Beginning in April 1928, however, the turbulence in the cities subsided, and it became evident that the CCP had for the time given up the struggle for power, and had gone into hiding in defeat. This change of tactics was the result of a Comintern conference held in Moscow in February, when there was adopted a new policy

for China, calling for the abandonment of efforts at
armed insurrection and the concentration of all
efforts on the organization of workers and peasants
through subterranean channels.[2] The revolutionaries
went back into the villages, where there were banditry,
poverty, and a sprinkling of revolutionary ideas, to
start their work afresh among the peasantry.

Chu Teh had been stationed in Nanchang at the
time of its capture by Ho Lung and Yeh T'ing in August
1927, and joined forces with those Reds in their drive
south toward Swatow and Canton. After the collapse of
the attempt to establish the seat of the Soviet
Government at the latter place, Chu Teh went into the
Fukien-Kiangsi border region with his troops, coming
out in April 1928 to establish a Soviet Government
at Chingkangshan (Kiangsi). Ho Lung and Yeh T'ing
retreated to the Haifeng-Lufeng region in eastern
Kuangtung and established in that agrarian background
village soviets that flourished for six months and were
never wholly eradicated, coming back strongly in 1930.[3]

Chu Teh next moved into western Kiangsi with his
army, capturing such important district towns as
Lingkon, Suichuan, and Yunhsien; the bandits in the
region of Pinghsiang, Liling, Anyuan, and Liuyang were
consolidated into his forces, which were then strong
enough to capture Chaling and Linghsien. The next step

2. Tokyo Report, "The Chinese Communist Party and the
   Soviet Russian Activities in Mongolia", February 1932,
   p 6.
3. No word has been heard of Yeh T'ing in recent years,
   and it is probable that he was killed in the fighting
   between the Reds and the regular troops in the Haifeng-
   Lufeng sector in 1928, or in some other conflict soon
   after. Ho Lung proceeded from Haifeng to the wild region
   comprising north-western Hunan and south-western Hupeh.

was consolidation with the group under Mao Tse-tung
(毛澤東) who had already occupied Chenchow,
Tzuhsin, and Leiyang, in Hunan. Chu Teh now acted
as the military commander of this heterogeneous
conglomeration of bandits, regular army units, and
remnants of the people's organizations that had been
forced under the tutelage of the Red Kuomintang; the
group was designated the 4th Red Army. Mao Tse-tung
acted as Political Officer for Chu Teh, as he has
done ever since. By the end of 1928, the area roamed
by this Army comprised some 20 districts in south and
eastern Hunan. As it went, there were organized Red
Guards and Youth Guards, and there were re-established
the laborers' and peasants' organizations, and the
women's associations, that had been destroyed by T'ang
Sheng-chih (唐生智). By January 1929 the strength
of the 4th Army had so grown that Ho Chien (何　鍵)
felt called upon to proceed in person to Pinghsiang,
Kiangsi, in his capacity of Commander-in-Chief of the
Bandit-Suppression Forces of Hunan and Kiangsi. As
the result of the combined pressure from the Hunanese
and some Kiangsi troops from Kanchow, Chu Teh's 4th
Army retreated south along the Hunan-Kiangsi border in
two sections, re-joining somewhere in the region about
Takeng (Kiangsi), which it captured. Reinforcements
for the Government armies forced the withdrawal of the
Red Army toward Fukien.

The year 1929 proved a busy one for the newly-
established Nanking Government. One by one - instead of
all together, as might have happened in a country less

torn by a jealous sectionalism revolts against the
Chiang-Soong control burst out in different parts of
the country, led successively by Li Tsung-jen
(李宗仁) and Pai Ch'ung-hsi (白崇禧), Feng
Yü-hsiang, Chang Fa-k'uei, and T'ang Sheng-chih.
As if internal troubles were not sufficient in number,
a quarrel was provoked with the U. S. S. R. out of
which China emerged an inglorious second-best.

Thus busily engaged in relegating more and more
of the former "Comrades" into the Opposition to the
accompaniment of accusations of Bolshevism and Soviet
connections, the Nanking group had neither the time nor
the money to spend upon what were still, for everybody,
"just bandits". This attitude constituted a very
considerable factor favoring the growth of the Red
groups. Chu Teh had grown in strength with the capture
of several important cities in the Fukien-Kiangsi border
area. P'eng Teh-huai (彭德懷) had risen into
prominence as the commander of the 5th Red Army by the
capture of Namyung, northern Kuangtung, on June 1, 1929,
after the looting of Kueiyang and Chenchow in Hunan.
Fang Chih-min (方志敏), who had left Nanchang in
1927 in company with Shao Shih-p'ing (邵式平) with
only 7 rifles between them, had become the leader of
the 10th Red Army, in north-eastern Kiangsi. Other
groups had a mushroom growth in the Yangtze Valley
provinces.

More important still, there was the growth of a
definite orientation of the guerilla groups. With the
evident increasing strength of the Red groups in the

course of the year, the CCP sent its agents into the
field for the knitting together of these scattered
groups, and for the directing of them into the proper
revolutionary path. The Chinese peasant has never
pretended - nor does he now - to a very high stage of
culture. From the available evidence relating to the
period immediately subsequent to the fall of the
Hankow Government it seems certain that, what with
their wounds smarting and their ranks filled with the
rag-and-bobtail of soldiery and outlaw bandits, the
first Red groups carried on their fight against the
existing order with an unrestrained savagery that
exercised but little discrimination in its incidence.
Much potential support was alienated by the Red
excesses. It cannot be said yet that the Reds of
China are kinder to their enemies than those enemies
are to them, but even as early as the beginning of
1930 they had become much more selective as regards
the sections of the population they stigmatized as
"enemies of the people". The discipline demanded by
a growing organization, and the practical political
need for the friendly support of the population in
the territory used as a long-time base for Red
military and political activities, soon forced an
important change in tactics. This was noted by an
able political observer early in 1930:

> "The communists today employ means other
> than violence and death. For two years Hai
> Fong and Lon Fong were occupied by brigands
> and terror reigned supreme; some merchants have
> been murdered and burned to death. However,
> for some months, according to what the people
> say who come from Hupeh and Kiangsi, the

communists have changed their methods, they
have commenced looking to the security of
the regions which they have been occupying
for a long time. The gentry alone are uneasy;
the people of good reputation and those who
do not resist are able to carry on peacefully.
Their incomes are derived from requisitions
and confiscations. Damages have been done,
but the communists no longer, as heretofore
without reason, kill the people and commit
incendiarism. The brigands which they command
are very well disciplined, if one is to believe
P'ong K'i Piao, who is in command of the
suppression of brigandage. The communists
actually refrain from stirring up the poor
against the rich. Everywhere they go they
immediately cancel debts, take off taxes and
apportion the land......The communists function
especially in the country districts, their
proselytes are peasants who resume their
customary tasks when the regular troops arrive.
All do not follow the communists, they remain
in their villages but the relations are not
broken...." The paper then adds: "Now, if the
civil war does not cease and the political
situation improve, the communist question will
become increasingly serious. For the future
of the country, this affair is more important
than the actual war in central China."4

The truth contained in the two last sentences is

becoming more evident each day.

The Government had few troops to spare to send

against the Reds, and no ability to put the national

polity "en bon chemin". But the force of the

propaganda organization was turned against the Reds,

as if to conjure them away by statements that it

should be so. On February 11, 1930, KUO WEN reported

that the Red troops under Chu Teh and Mao Tse-tung

were still holding several districts in Kiangsi,

"although they were surrounded on all sides by

government forces"; on February 27th, Mao Tse-tung

was reported as having died of tuberculosis in January,

4. JOURNAL DE PEKIN, April 23 (?), 1930.

at Lungyen, Fukien; and on March 17th it was disclosed
that "The military authorities in Hupeh and Hunan have
decided to suppress the bandits in their areas within
six months". The Reds had again come into the public
eye. The revolutionary movement that had been thrown
back south in 1927 and then back to the villages in
the hinterland, was surging up in new strength.

During February, the battle between Yen Hsi-shan
(閻錫山) and Chiang Kai-shih had been one of
telegrams of a mutually recriminatory nature. With
strained relations between the Kuangsi and Kuangtung
factions, the Communists captured Lungchow, Poseh, and
Tapingfu. In March, the division of the country into
two hostile camps, North versus Nanking, became more
definite; and, some 10,000 Red troops under Chu Teh
got control in the north-west part of Kiangsi, while
other bands held power as before in the region from
Kanchow to Kian. Concerning the operations of the
Reds, the Legation remarked in its Monthly Political
Report that the moves evidently had certain political
significance, besides motives of personal gain, "as
the populace was not interfered with, only Government
buildings being destroyed."

Heavy fighting in Honan between the Northern Allies
and Nanking did not begin until May, when the Communist
control in Kiangsi became almost complete; any troops
that might have constituted a bulwark against the Red
drive had been thrown into the fray against Feng's
troops. P'eng Teh-huai's army took Yochow on July 3,
1930, and various important district cities were captured

by different Communist bands in Hupeh and Anhui. On
July 28th, some 10,000 Red troops under Ho Lung, P'eng
Teh-huai, and Chu Teh (?), captured the provincial
capital Changsha, thoroughly looting the place. They
established a Soviet Government there on August 1st
for the provinces of Hunan, Hupeh, and Kiangsi. With
the aid of American, Italian, and Japanese gunboats,
Ho Chien re-took the city on August 5th. Then, although
the place had been badly looted already, he demanded a
large sum of money from the merchants, "to keep the
troops from looting".

In the North, the "Enlarged Plenary Session of the
Central Headquarters of the Kuomintang of China" met
in Peiping on July 13th. Three weeks before, on May
20th, the First Soviet Congress for the Soviet Districts
of China had met in Shanghai, under the leadership of
the CCP and the All-China Labor Federation (ACLF), for
the discussion of political policy and fighting tactics
for the Soviet groups. The program of the Soviet
Government was laid down, laws issued concerning land
and labor, and a decision reached about military
tactics of the Red armies. Another revolutionary
movement of revolt was to be organized, with the aim
of meeting the endless civil wars with the capture of
power in one or a number of provinces to hasten the
desired victory of the Soviet Power in the whole of China.[5]

5. (INTERNATIONAL PRESS CORRESPONDENCE, No. 51, p. 1051)
   In May also, the JOURNAL DE PEKIN noted that "Les
   campagnes chinoises passent rapidement du coté des
   communistes. Il y a six mois, ce mouvement était peu
   important, on le considérait comme négligeable..."

The establishment of the Peiping "National Government" on September 1, 1930, was not sufficient to off-set the serious defeat Yen Hsi-shan's armies had suffered at Tsinan on August 15th, and on September 18th Chang Hsueh-liang (張學良) issued his circular telegram calling for the cessation of hostilities. The vanguard of the Manchurian troops reached Peiping on September 22nd, and the war was over. Excepting, that the effects of its devastation remained in the lives of the people, and the country was further impoverished. So too was the Government, whom the war had cost over $200,000,000 while the North had spent about one-half as much. The total indebtedness of the country was about $4 billion.

With the internal conditions of the country in such disorder, the Second All-China Conference of the International Organization for the Assistance of Revolution (MOPR) met at Shanghai in August. Forty-five persons attended, including delegates from the Chinese Red Army, the Revolutionary Students' League, and the Red Labor unions. There, **and** at the congress of the Trade Union International (PROFINTERN) in Moscow about the same time, it was decided that a Soviet Government for the whole of China had become a practical possibility. Since the middle of 1930, the energies of the Communist organization in China have been concentrated on the task of achievement of this goal.

2. First Punitive Expedition (December 1930 to January 1931).

In September, the combined armies of P'eng Teh-huai and Chu Teh attempted to again capture Changsha, but

were successfully repulsed by Ho Chien. Chu Teh
retired with his troops to Kiangsi once more, while
P'eng went back to his old haunts around Liuyang and
Pinghsiang. The practical cessation of war in the
North made it possible for somewhat more attention
to be paid to the threat within, and Ho Ying-ch'in
(何 應 欽) was made Commander-in-Chief of Bandit
Suppression. It was reported that

> "The government forces of the three provinces
> (Hunan, Hupeh, Kiangsi - EC) were concentrating
> on the Hunan-Kiangsi borders in preparation for
> a campaign to surround and extirpate the Red
> remnants once and for all."[6]

The Government was said to have advanced 12 divisions
for operations against the Reds - 6 into Hupeh, 2 into
Anhui, and 4 into Kiangsi.

Kian was captured by the Reds on October 4, 1930,
with considerable looting and killing in the city by
the "little peasant" soviets before the arrival of
Chu Teh and P'eng Teh-huai with 20,000 troops brought
order. A soviet government was established there, and
the Red position consolidated by the prompt capture
shortly afterwards of Tungku, Ining, Hoping, Hokow, and
Kingtehchen;[7] in Hunan province, Huajung, Changteh,

6. ASIATIC, September 28, 1930.
7. Kingtehchen, which fell to the Reds three times in
   the course of 1930, suffered a loss to its industry
   of more than $10,000,000. Its porcelain workers
   are all scattered, it being said that some 10,000
   were forced to accompany the Reds when they left.
   The porcelain industry of this place is supposed to
   have persisted for more than 900 years, but it is
   now bankrupt. There are not more than 10% of the
   kilns that have resumed operations, and the financial
   interests that are really the foundation of the
   Kingtehchen pottery industry are also suffering under
   the stringency of their circumstances, so that what
   with the various imposts business is at a standstill.
   (TA KUNG PAO, April 16, 1931)

Hsinchow, and Nanhsien were captured, Ho Lung playing
a very active part. In Hupeh, the Reds were in Kienli
and Kingchow. At the end of September, 21 foreigners
were being held for ransom in the Hankow consular
district. Kian was captured in mid-November, and,
with Chu Teh holding that place, the position of the
regular troops stationed at Kishui, almost directly
across the Kan River, might have been thought to be
considerably imperilled. But, according to reports,
the troops under Teng were content to gaze complacently
on the red flag flying on the opposite bank, and to
fraternize with the Red Army and sell it ammunition
equipment. Soon after mid-November, when it became
noised about that Chu Teh was going to advance on
Kishui, General Teng in conjunction with Magistrate
P'eng decided to evacuate the city. Entreated by the
local gentry to stay, they said that they would need
$800,000 with which to "encourage the troops" - and
they compromised on $200,000. Teng then declared
strict martial law, prohibiting people from going out
on the streets at night, and ordered that all boats on
the river should be tied up at a specified place at
night on the river "so that they might not be stolen
by the Reds". The next morning, General Teng,
Magistrate P'eng, the money, and troops, had all
disappeared. So, too, it turned out, had the boats.
Chu and Mao arrived and took over the city.[8]

Chiang Kai-shih himself pushed the campaign against
the Reds with considerable energy. KUO WEN reported on
December 5th that the orders of the Central Government

---

8. TA KUNG PAO, January 17, 1931.

were to the effect that all towns in the hands of the
Communists should be recaptured within a period of 1½
months, failing which the commanders concerned were
to be punished "as in the case of disobedience". On
November 29th, Chiang had issued a circular order to
the several army units concerned, directing that:

(a) There shall be no delay in carrying out orders
    or wilful withdrawal contrary to instructions;
(b) Troops shall not buy off outlaws with money or
    munitions, and secret sales of equipment by
    individual soldiers must stop;
(c) Soldiers must not molest the inhabitants,
    extort money from them, or interfere with the
    local administration;
(d) Troops must not incorporate bandits into their
    units, or even new recruits from the locality
    where they are stationed;
(e) Negligence or treason resulting in failure to
    protect a locality against outlaws will be
    severely punished;
(f) The higher officers will be directly responsible
    to the Generalissimo for their conduct, and
    meritorious work on the part of officers and
    men will be liberally rewarded.

These regulations indicated where the weaknesses of the
Government troops lay.

Three Pacification Commissioners were appointed -
one each for the Honan-Shensi-Shansi Border, the Honan-
Hupeh-Anhui Border, and the Hunan-Kiangsi Border. On
December 9th, Chiang summoned his several generals to
his resident headquarters at Nanchang for a conference
concerning the anti-Red campaign. As a result of this
conference, there was issued the offer of rewards of
$50,000 each for the capture of Chu Teh, Mao Tse-tung,
Huang Kung-luoh (黃公畧), and P'eng Teh-huai; there
was broadcast to the Red troops the offer of reward to
each Red soldier surrendering with equipment - $30 if
with a rifle, $500 if with a machine-gun, and $1,000
when turning over with a field-gun. On December 10, 1930,

the Central Government issued a mandate stating that
Communists and bandits should be suppressed "within
three or six months at most". Lu Ti-p'ing (魯 滌 平)
meeting Chiang in Nanking, swore that, if the Reds
were not exterminated within three months, he would
take off his head beneath the country's flag in
sacrifice; and, he asked for several more divisions
of troops.

Concrete results were not long in forthcoming.
Late in December, Kian was reported taken from the
Reds, with great slaughter by the regular troops and
important captures of munitions. Government circles
were greatly elated at what was considered a very
important victory, it being pointed out that Kian
was the main base of the rebel strength, the Red
capital of Soviet China (and had been, as a matter of
fact, for 45 days). But something suddenly happened,
and the whole story of the affair came out slowly
through other sources. Upon hearing of Chiang Kai-shih's
well-advertised "campaign of extermination", Chu Teh
had called a meeting of the population of Kian and told
the people that although he did not fear Chiang's armies
he preferred to conserve his strength; he asked for a
vote on the question of whether he should go, or stay
and fight. Getting no answer from the frightened people,
he again put the question, stating that if he got no
answer he would kill them all. They voted that he go,
and he left with his troops for Tungku within three days,
taking with him at the same time the machinery of the

factories, oil, salt, fuel, and rice. Lu Ti-p'ing walked in the gates and reported his victory to the Central Government.

Lu Ti-p'ing had advanced on December 29th and 30th with four divisions; the 50th, 25th, 47th, and 18th. When the Reds began the retreat to Tungku, they drew the 50th into the hills and lost them. The 18th entered Tungku under Chang Hui-tsan (張輝瓚) on December 31st, and indulged themselves generally in looting and crapulence. It was while they were thus celebrating New Year's Eve that the Reds returned in force. Chang's troops had no chance of coming out of their bewildered state, and were easily beaten down and disarmed. They were then each offered $20 per month by their captors in the event they wished to serve in the Red Army; or, each was given $3 travelling expenses if he wished to return to his home. The Red Army then dressed in the uniforms of the 18th, took their flags, and went out to meet the 50th, upon which they were able to open fire at close range and kill or wound about half before the regular troops were aware of what was happening. Chang Hui-tsan himself died either by skinning alive or being cut slowly into bits (凌遲), and his head was sent down the river on a plank on which were written various ribald remarks (the authorities gave him a wooden body and a funeral such as his rank merited). At the same time, Ningtu, which had been evacuated by the Reds as were Kian and Tungku, was re-taken by Chu Teh's forces, the command

of T'an Tao-yuan (譚道源) being defeated. Chang
Hui-tsan had with him only two brigades. The third
was downstream, not having yet arrived at Lungkang;
hearing in good time of the battle at Tungku, this
third brigade was able to preserve itself intact.
Chu Shao-liang (朱紹良) and his two divisions
under Mao Ping-wen (毛炳文) and Hsu K'o-hsiang
(許克祥) stayed in Nanfeng after the debacle,
afraid to stir out of the gates; Lu Ti-p'ing was still
in Kian, K'ung Ho-ch'ung (孔荷寵) and some small
bands of Reds suddenly returned from Hupeh and took
Kaoan and Shangkao, thus further releasing the pressure
on Chu Teh. Shao Shih-p'ing took Jaocheng. Wuning,
Ifeng, and Nihuang also fell to the Reds, before
mid-January. Lu Ti-p'ing, under the pretence of
"strengthening the defences of the province", fearfully
rushed back to Nancheng. Chiang Kai-shih was enraged
at the pusillanimity of his generals, but was forced
to throw Wang Chin-yü (王金鈺) and Hsu Yuan-ch'üan
(徐源泉) into western Kiangsi, while Sun Lien-chung
(孫連仲) was ordered to south Kiangsi with all his
force "to trample flat the Red Army's heart". The
death of Chang Hui-tsan and his command had demoralized
the anti-Red army, and the TA KUNG PAO remarked that
the Government strength consisted of one thin battle
line, and the hope that the Reds would "sit themselves
to death."[9]

The situation at the beginning of 1931 was likewise
not of the best elsewhere. From Hunan, it was reported

9. TA KUNG PAO, January 17, January 21, February 23,
February 27, 1931.

that Chaling and Yuhsien still remained in the hands
of the 3-4000 Reds under Ch'en Shao (陳　韶) and
Liu Shih-yun (劉 沛 雲). "The troops for the
suppression of banditry merely go around the edge of
the city making a lot of noise, and that's all". Ho
Chien was described as a tiger rider (騎虎之勢),
despised by Chiang Kai-shih who knew Ho's impotence
but kept him on for want of a better man to keep
Hunan in the Chiang-Soong sphere of influence. The
Reconstruction Commission was stigmatized as a corrupt
body wholly interested in raking in funds and quite
bare of concrete accomplishments; their latest proposal
was to collect $20 per picul on opium. As regards the
Pingkiang region, it was remarked that "the more the
army exterminates the Reds, the more Reds there are".[10]

This period marked the end of the first expedition,
the Reds being left victorious. The reasons for the
failure of the anti-Red campaign in this period were,
according to the Chinese press, as follows: 1) war-
weary troops were sent in, with officers who were too
cocky over their success against Feng Yü-hsiang and
Yen Hsi-shan to fight; 2) the people of the province,
disappointed and betrayed by the Provincial Government,
had lost their faith in it and refused to cooperate;
3) there was no definite military plan; 4) the Government
depended upon military strength alone in their attempt
to beat the Reds.[11]

---

10. TA KUNG PAO, January 6, January 21.
11. TA KUNG PAO, January 22, 1931.

There may be added two more: 1) there was evidently the deep-seated suspicion among certain of the troops that they were being sent into Kiangsi chiefly to be gotten out of the way; 2) the hostile territory, with its wild mountainous terrain, favored the guerilla fighters who knew every path and hiding-place of the country and had the support of the population, which was definitely antipathetic toward the Government armies, as intimated by the TA KUNG PAO (see above). This situation was outlined by General Tai Yueh (戴　岳), a brigade commander under Lu Ti-p'ing, in a pamphlet on the subject of the anti-Red campaign, two of his six reasons for the failure of the drive being as follows:

> "(4) the mismanagement and incompetence of the hsien magistrates; the inefficiency of the police who disturbed the people instead of protecting them; the local gentry who fatten themselves on the people by oppressing them, combined to drive the people to the arms of the Communists; (6) bankrupt condition of the peasantry, unemployment among the artisans and workers, and the general economic distress among the people supply inexhaustible fuel to the growth of Communism.[12]

At this time, there were about 150,000 Government troops in Kiangsi, stretched along a front demarcated by Loan, Yungfeng, Kishui, Kian, Hsingkuo, and Kanchow. Chiang Kai-shih launched the second wave of the anti-Red Forces, calling for the completion of the suppression campaign within four months, by the end of April, at the latest; there would be special rewards for finishing the job ahead of time, but under no circumstances could the limit be exceeded.

_____

12. Yang Chien, "Communist Menace in China", CENTRAL CHINA POST, July 20 ult. seq., 1931.

3. Second Punitive Expedition (February-June 1931).

Ho Ying-ch'in left for Kiangsi on February 2, 1931, to start action in his capacity of Commander-in-Chief of the second anti-Red campaign. The Reds made public the prices they usually paid for munitions bought from the regular troops: $80 per rifle, $100 per pistol, $500 per machine-gun. These bids were higher than those offered by the Central Government, and, moreover, the Reds stated that any soldier wishing to desert the Government forces and return to his home would be protected on his way and the safety of his family and relatives guaranteed; contrariwise, the families of regular troops hailing from Kiangsi and Hunan were, it was promised, to be exterminated in the event such soldiers did not desert.[13]

Ho Ying-ch'in's campaign did not proceed rapidly. On March 3rd, he reported from Nanchang that his troops had killed 20,000 Reds, "but inasmuch as an equal number of Government troops turned over to them the Reds really suffered no material loss".[14] Chiang Kuang-nai (蔣 光 鼐) proceeded from Kuangtung into southern Kiangsi, and Wang Chin-yü was ordered down into the same region. Chiang Kai-shih, to counter-act the Red virus, sent a propaganda corps into Kiangsi to instruct the people in the reasons why they should oppose the Reds instead of the Government. Sun Lien-chung's 30,000 troops, after a considerable procrastination

---

13. RENGO, February 3, 1931.
14. RENGO, March 3, 1931.

which enabled Sun to make certain that he and his
ex-Kuominchün command would be properly provided
for in Kiangsi, finally arrived at their positions
in that province. Despite the current rumor that
Ch'en Chi-t'ang (陳 濟 棠) had ordered the recall
of his two divisions of the 19th Route Army from
Kiangsi for political reasons, Ho Ying-ch'in ordered
that a general attack should be begun on the Communists
on March 21st.

Ho Ying-ch'in pooh-poohed the idea that the Reds
were anything to be afraid of, stating at the weekly
memorial service at Nanchang that

> "They are but a bunch of crows (i.e., a motley
> crowd easily scattered - EC) - disgruntled
> soldiers and middle-school students who have
> failed to graduate... They want nothing more
> than to satisfy their animal lasciviousness...
> a bunch of lazy vagrants."

They had, he said, but one or two thousand good rifles
and a few home-made guns; the sum of their guns in all
the provinces would not reach 20,000, with no more than
20 bullets per rifle. "The extermination of the Red
bandits is before our eyes, and the people not only need
not be fearful, but may trust the troops to protect
them."[15] For the two months subsequent to the death of
Chang Hui-tsan, the 14 or 15 divisions in Kiangsi had
been sitting motionless on the Kian-Linchuan and Kian-
Fengcheng lines, not daring to stir from their tracks.
The addition of the 2 divisions and 1 brigade of Sun
Lien-chung's troops, and the deploying of them in the
direction of the concentration of Red strength at Ningtu,

15. TA KUNG PAO, March 24, 1931.

considerably brightened the spirits of the massed
Government armies (now totalling 200,000 men) that
were to wipe out the ragged "bunch of crows" -
despite the apparent fact that Sun's troops had no
great ardor for the task. Chiang Kai-shih, so that
none should have any doubts that he was not fighting
a political group, on March 24th ordered that the
enemy should no longer be dignified by the title
"fei-kung" (匪共 - Communist rebels) but should
thenceforth be termed "ch'ih-fei" (赤匪 - Red bandits).
And on March 24th it was reported that $700,000 had
been sent to Ho Ying-ch'in from Nanking as the first
installment of the war fund.[16] Chiang Kai-shih gave
Ho Ying-ch'in strict orders that the Kiangsi-Hunan-Hupeh
Reds should be subjugated before the convocation of the
People's Convention (May 2, 1931). On April 1st the
Headquarters of the Generalissimo issued strict orders
along these lines to the commanders of the several
forces engaged in Kiangsi, holding them strictly
accountable for the extermination of the Reds within
the time limit set.

Meanwhile, in the Hunan-Hupeh-Honan sector, there
had been important happenings. About March 1st, 10,000
soldiers (many of whom had formerly served under Wang
Lou-wu (王老五) and Fan Chung-hsiu (樊鍾秀) of

---

16. It was at about this time, according to a RENGO
report, that the Finance Bureau had expressed
itself as unable, because of an empty Treasury, to
comply with Chiang Kai-shih's order to send $100,000
to Ho Ying-ch'in with which to stir the martial
ardor of the troops; Chiang was reported as being
very displeased with this reply, and as ordering
the unfortunate Bureau to raise $20,000,000 for the
campaign in short order.

the 12th Division under Yuan Ying (袁 英) mutinied
at Hsintien, on the Ping-Han Railway in southern Honan,
presumably because they believed that they were going
to be disarmed and disbanded. Liulin was captured by
the mutineers on March 2nd. The area is one where the
Reds have been strong for several years, and, allegedly
reinforced by several thousand Reds, the revolting
troops tore up some 30 li of railway track and occupied
the whole area between Hsinyang and Wushengkuan,
capturing Kuangshui. A brigade of troops despatched
from Wuhan to Liulin for their suppression joined up
with the rebels, and the important pass of Wushenkuan
itself was threatened. Two divisions of troops were
rushed down from Honan, and three more despatched from
Hupeh, including the 34th Division under Yueh Wei-chün
(岳 維 峻). But Yueh Wei-chün's 10,000 men also
turned over to the Reds at Hsiaohochi, and Yueh himself
never returned.[17] The Reds operating against Kuangshui
were chiefly those under K'Uang Chi-hsun (曠 繼 勛)
and Wang I-nan (汪 以 南). The Government troops
finally drove back the Red armies and revolting troops,
re-capturing Liulin on March 5th. According to the
UNITED PRESS, 50,000 regular troops were engaged in the
battle. The remnants of the lost 12th and 34th Divisions
were reorganized.

---

17. It is reported by missionaries that he is still alive,
and, coming of a fairly well-to-do family, proves to
be a valuable "jou-p'iao" (肉 票 - meat ticket), the
Reds valuing him at $100,000; moreover, he enjoys the
status of semi-privileged military adviser to the
Honan-Hupeh-Anhui Soviet Government, upon request
speaking against the evils of militarism to Red mass
meetings. Bert Nelson is held by the same group, but
it is not known whether he acts in any advisory
capacity.

At that time, the Soviet Government for the Honan-Anhui-Hupeh Border 豫鄂皖蘇維埃政府) was situated at Chiliping, in North-east Hupeh, under the Chairmanship of Cheng Hsing-wei (鄭行為), and the chief Red military strength of the three provinces was concentrated in that region. In fact, the whole Red strength of the three provinces was probably as great as that of Kiangsi. And, besides, in Honan, there were some 100,000 bandits, mostly troop remnants or deserters, equipped with rifles.

On March 21, 1931, the date Ho Ying-ch'in had set for the beginning of the general advance on the Reds, the Reorganization Committee met in Nanchang to settle upon the measures of administrative reorganization which should be taken in the areas that were to be re-captured from the Communists. The general plan entailed the cooperation, in the several districts, of Tangpu (Kuomintang Branch), district government, and the local reorganization committee, with the organization of the local militia in every case within two months. A few days later, the Central Government issued orders that all districts in the provinces of Hunan, Hupeh, Honan, Anhui, Kiangsi, Chekiang, and Fukien, were to organize local volunteer corps, and effect the system of "Pao-chia" (保甲 - mutual guarantee), before August 1st, in order to assist in the furtherance of the anti-Red campaign.

Ho Ying-ch'in's order for the general advance was issued on April 1st. On April 4th, Chiang issued an order granting to commanders in the campaign permission to recruit to make up for any losses the troops might suffer, thus relieving the fears raised by his previous

order (that there should be <u>no</u> recruiting) that heavy
losses would leave those military commanders' political
positions impaired. The achievements of the Government
troops after the date first announced for the beginning
of the drive, March 21st, were immediate and outstanding.
KUO MIN reported on March 30th that Chiang Kuang-nai
had taken Wanan and Chungyi, Yuan Shao-ch'ang (袁紹昌)
captured Huangfeng, T'an Tao-yuan took Shoushui and
T'ungku; the districts of Chungjen, Ihuang, Lohan,
Yungfeng, and Ninghsing, had been cleared of Reds. On
April 3rd, the same agency gave Lu Ti-p'ing's report
that the entire area between Kian and Kanchow had been
cleared of Reds; also, Chiang Kuang-nai had captured
Lungkang on April 2nd, and the 60th Division under
Ts'ai T'ing-k'ai (蔡廷楷) had raided a Communist
organ at Hsingkuo (not captured until four months
later - EC) and captured some Red literature; and, as
regarded the situation in Hupeh and Hunan, "As a result
of the tireless efforts of the Government troops, no
large outlaw horde now exists in the two provinces".
It was also considered a mark of the degree of the
Government's success that P'eng Teh-huai and Huang
Kung-lueh had signified their desire to surrender
and that Huang had sent his mother and wife to Changsha
as hostages, as a guarantee of his good faith (RENGO:
the wives and <u>children</u> of both were sent).

Nanking reported that Chu Teh had been defeated,
and was fleeing toward Kukeng with something over 10,000
rifles, seeking to escape into Hunan; the Reds were said

to be short of provisions and facing starvation.[18] Ho
Ying-ch'in issued an order directing that people
might not pay ransom for any captives held by the
Communists, for the Government forces would set all
captives free by the end of April at the latest,
"when the outlaws will be completely rounded up in
Kiangsi". He ordered the several commanders to
capture all Red territories by that time. "Latest
reports from the front state that the Red gangs are
now fleeing into the Fukien borders where chaos is
prevailing."[19] The 19th Route Army disarmed 8,000
Communists in the region of Kanchow, and the wife of
a prominent Red commander turned over 1,000 Red troops
to the authorities, according to reports, thus
accounting for 9,000 of the 1-2,000 armed Communists
(see above) said by Ho Ying-ch'in to constitute the
Red forces, besides the many dead and wounded.

Huang Kung-lueh and P'eng Teh-huai did not turn
up. This was said to have been the result of Huang's
changing his mind about surrendering to the Government
as he had agreed with P'eng, whereupon P'eng killed
him and disarmed his troops.[20] But P'eng didn't show
up either, and although asseverations and rumors
continued until July, neither Huang nor P'eng arrived

18. TA KUNG PAO, April 6, 1931.
19. ASIATIC, April 9, 1931.
20. UNITED PRESS, April 10, 1931.

in the Government camp.[21]

About the middle of April 1931, there spread
throughout the country the alarm that the Communists,
in a desperate effort to embroil the Central Government
with the Powers, were planning an uprising throughout
the country on April 20th, when they would enter upon
a general program of destruction of foreign property
and foreign lives. The plot had been discovered by
Wang Chin-yü and, as the time drew near, the authorities
took strict precautions, military law was proclaimed in
the important cities, and the foreign representatives
were warned of the danger that threatened. But the day
passed without a ripple. Nanchang despatches of April
15th reported the completion of the first part of the
anti-Red campaign as formulated by Ho Ying-ch'in, with
the rounding up of the scattered bands of Reds along

21. There seems to have been a certain amount of
    plausibility about the story of the turnover of
    Huang and P'eng. They both had their homes in
    Siangtan, Hunan, and the family of Huang was still
    there - had never left, in fact. At the time of
    the attempted invasion of Li Tsung-jen in 1930,
    there were then also stories circulated that both
    Huang and P'eng, and especially the former, were
    making sheep's eyes in the direction of Li, and it
    seems probable that there was even the sending of
    Huang's emissaries to Li with proposals concerning
    the conditions of the turnover, but the project
    fell through when Li retreated back into Kuangsi.
    In the 1931 case of Huang and P'eng, there is the
    possibility that Ho Chien took Huang's family into
    custody in order to bring pressure to bear upon
    the Reds and force a turnover (it is interesting
    to note that most Chinese militarists would rather
    have a hard-fighting rebel or bandit in their own
    army then dead). At any rate, Huang's uncle,
    Huang Han-hsiang (黃漢湘) evidently made
    several trips as a go-between, on at least one
    occasion carrying Ho Chien money to Huang Kung-lueh.
    But, although the money may have been actually paid,
    the purchase fell through. It may have been a gross
    swindle, it may have been provocation, or it may
    have all been a mare's nest from the beginning.

both banks of the Kan River and in central Kiangsi in

the Kian-Kishui region; the second part of the program

called for the capture of Kuangchang and Tungku; and

> "In the third and final stage of the bandit-
> suppression programme which is expected to be
> effected during the latter part of the month,
> house-to-house searches will be instituted in
> the various districts so as to prevent the
> bandits from hiding among peaceful citizens
> and to remove the bandit menace once for all."

KUO MIN then reported that Kuangchang was captured by

Mao Ping-wen on April 15th, with the killing or

capturing of 2,000 Reds and capturing large stores of

amunition; "The second stage of the suppression

programme for Kiangsi is concluded, it is announced",

for Kuangchang was the last stronghold of the Reds

in southeastern Kiangsi - Futien, Paisha, Lungkang,

Taokang, Peitung, Kuangchang, Hotsun, Hsinfeng,

Menghsien, having all been captured from the Communists.

Chu Teh was reported as having abandoned Yütu and fled

to Juichin. In Hupeh, Hsu Yuan-ch'üan set a time limit

of three months for the completion of the job of bandit

suppression.

On April 20th, the TA KUNG PAO reported that "The

militia[22] are only ten li from Kuangchang, and it is

expected that the capture of the city can soon be

announced." The Reds were reported as having all fled

to Ningtu and Shihcheng, where they were surrounded.

---

22. The battle-order in the advance of Government troops
   is ordinarily: 1) peasant groups such as the Red
   Spears, 2) local militia, 3) regular troops. Thus,
   for the militia to be ten li from Kuangchang would
   not necessarily indicate that the Government armies
   were close. It may be remarked that the advance of
   the Red troops is along similar lines, as: 1) peasant
   fighters, 2) Red Guards, 3) Red troops.

Lo Lin (羅林) reported from Taian that he discovered
the military plans of the Reds (in general, to concentrate
the entire Red military strength of central China in
Kiangsi); moreover, since Huang Kung-luoh and P'eng Teh-
huai had become an opposition party in the Red camp, the
task was rendered easier still, "and the whole lot of
them can soon be exterminated."[23] The Nanchang Headquarters reported that the Reds had fallen into dis-
agreement, with the consequent destruction of the
Soviet organization, and that their armies were fighting
each other.[24] However, a discordant note crept into the
epic of Government victories. A Nanchang correspondent
of the NORTH CHINA DAILY NEWS wrote on April 15th that
it was evident that the Reds had, with the entry of
Ho Ying-ch'in and Sun Lien-chung into Kiangsi, split
their forces into small guerilla bands and adopted the
policy of avoiding the main Government forces; hence,

> "The Government forces up to now have not fought
> serious battles with the Red armies, on account
> of the fact that, wherever the troops appear, the
> Reds, instead of standing up against them, try
> to run somewhere where there are few or no
> government forces."

In the Hupeh sector, Tuan Teh-ch'ang (段 德昌) had
been driven from Huajung (Hunan) by the troops under
Chang Ying (張 英) on March 24th (25th?), and
Hsu Yuan-ch'üan had previously re-captured Shihshou and
Ouchihkou. Tuan Teh-ch'ang was driven north into the
Taohua Mountains, which are a natural fortress, where he
was besieged by the troops under Hsu Yuan-ch'üan. But

23. TA KUNG PAO, April 25, 1931.
24. TA KUNG PAO, May 2, 1931.

Ho Lung began to move in western Hupeh. Leaving his
old haunts in the districts of Enshih and Haofeng in
early April, he marched north, capturing and looting
in rapid succession Patung, Tzukuei, Hsingshan, Yuan-an,
Tangyang, and Kingmen. Besides clearing out all the
provisions and material wealth of those places, he
augmented his military equipment with the arms and
munitions of the local militia. Hsu Yuan-ch'üan moved
quickly up-river to protect Ichang and Shasi; the Wuhan
Garrison Headquarters on April 21st announced a reward
of $100,000 for the marauder, dead or alive. On the
15th of the month, a general attack had been launched
on Tuan Teh-ch'ang's position in the Taohua Mountains,
five divisions of regular troops constituting the land
force, while gunboats were stationed along the river
to prevent the Reds from crossing over in the Kienli
region. However, the end of the attack saw Tuan still
lodged in his mountain fastness, while it was reported
that the Government forces had suffered heavy losses.[25]
The Wuhan Garrison Headquarters on April 29th reported
that Ho Lung's army had been annihilated, with 1,800
Red soldier prisoners of the beaten army "decapitated
without delay"; Ho Ying-ch'in at the weekly memorial
service at Nanchang reported that the Reds in southern
Kiangsi were in a corner, surrounded, "and the day when
they will be slaughtered is before our eyes". He also
noted that the people of the countryside were glad to
act as guides for the Government troops, and to spy for

----

25. TA KUNG PAO, April 27, 1931.

them; and, besides, there was dissension in the Red
camp, and Huang Kung-lueh and P'eng Teh-huai were
negotiating with the Government for their surrender,
so that the whole thing was splitting up.[26] On May
12, 1931, he submitted a report to the People's
Convention, "predicting that they would wipe out the
bandits within three months." Li Ming-chung (李鳴鐘),
Pacification Commissioner for the Honan-Hupeh-Anhui
Borders, expected to suppress all the south Honan Reds
within a month,[27] and Chi Hung-ch'ang (吉鴻昌)
shortly afterwards reported to Li (who had ordered
Chi Hung-ch'ang, Chang Yin-hsiang (張印相), Ko
Yun-lung (葛雲龍), Fan Hsi-chi (范熙績), Hsia
Tou-yin (夏斗寅), and Hsiao Chih-ch'u (蕭之楚)
into north-eastern Hupeh to cooperate with Chao Kuan-
t'ao (趙觀濤) and Tai Min-ch'üan (戴民權) for
a general attack against the Red area) that the Soviet
Government for that area had been destroyed, together
with the village Soviets, and important members of the
Soviet organization executed;

> "1) Concerning the Honan-Hupeh-Anhui Reds occupying
> Popiho, Hsinchi, Chiliping, Hsuanhuatien, comprising
> the 1st, 14th, 15th Armies, the 3rd Independent
> Division, and a Guard Brigade, amounting to 40-
> 50,000 men; all the peasants of that area have
> become Red slaves. 2) In accordance with orders,
> beginning on April 22nd, the 30th, 31st, 23rd
> Divisions battled the Red bandits and Red slaves
> for a decade at Popiho, Huwan, Hsinchi, Shuangshan,
> Changchienchangho, Yuanshukang, Chiliping, Kufengling,
> Huangpeichen, and Hsuanhuatien; these places have
> all been occupied, and the territory amounts to 600
> square li, the while the Reds have fled toward Anhui.
> 3) 6-7,000 Reds were killed in action, including a
> Red divisional commander and a captain. There were

26. TA KUNG PAO, April 27, 1931.
27. NORTH CHINA DAILY NEWS correspondent,
    May 2, 1931.

captured 287, including many women soldiers;
all have been executed. 4) Large amount of
munitions were captured. 5) The Government
forces lost a captain, a lieutenant, 4 corporals,
and 172 soldiers; there were over 40 of the
militia killed."[28]

But these oft-told tales had a cracked ring. The
People's Conference adopted a resolution concerning the
question of Communism in China. It concluded that,

"If the scourge of the Red bandits is as stated
in the Government's Red-extermination reports
(presumably some confidential reports depicting
the situation as it really existed - EC), it is
not only sufficient to overthrow the political
administration of our country, but it is enough
to destroy the social system of our country, cut
off our people's existence, wipe out the people of
our nation, and threaten the existence of our race.
This great calamity concerns all the people of the
whole country, and high and low of the country
must give their efforts in a cooperative effort
to destroy it."[29]

About the middle of May, after the close of the People's
Conference, the Nanchang Headquarters issued a proclamation:

"PROCLAMATION: Whereas it is known that the hearts
of the Red bandits are mad, that they receive the
gold of Soviet Russia, that they engage in traitorious
activities, that they delude our people, that they
are destroying our State, people with public spirit
are without exception energized. With the large army
now moving forward to strafe them, it is easy to point
out the day of their extinction. Considering the
fomentation of disorder and the doing of evil, there
are a few of the chief leaders who must be dealt with
in accordance with the gravity of their offences.
Because of this it is to be clearly stated that, with
the exception of a small number of bandit leaders,
whose offences cannot be pardoned, all the rest,
regardless of whether they are Red bandits, or Red
Guards, et cetera, if they will bring their weapons
and give themselves up, or repent their misdeeds and
accuse themselves, it is permissible to absolve them
of their misdeeds and let bygones be bygones, laying
the way open for their rehabilitation. If the bandits
may be got rid of, or meritorious services be performed,
even greater rewards must be granted, in accordance
with the circumstances. Our people, take notice of
this urgent proclamation."[30]

---

28. TA KUNG PAO, May 16, 1931.
29. TA KUNG PAO, May 5, 1931.
30. TA KUNG PAO, May 20, 1931.

On May 18th, the Hankow Headquarters of the Commander-in-Chief issued a "Table of Rewards and Punishments", of which the first three paragraphs promised suitable rewards to those giving certain assistance toward the suppression of the "Communist-bandits"; the two final paragraphs were:

> "4. Whoever harbours any 'Red' bandits will be liable to punishment as a Communist bandit. 5. Where any person is found guilty of (1) obstructing or tampering with the activities of any of the officers of the bandit-suppression forces, or (2) of plundering the provisions or the military supplies of the army, or (3) of destroying military telegraph wires or posts, the entire inhabitants of the village to which the offender belongs will be held jointly responsible for the offense."[31]

It is pertinent to remark that the common punishment for the offenses for which the population is thus given vicarious responsibility is death.

In Kiangsi, the Government troops had been closing in on the Reds until the latter occupied little more than five districts. The 5th Army, consisting of four Hupeh divisions, had closed in on Tungku, and the city was taken by Kung Ping-fan (公秉藩) on May 17th. P'eng Teh-huai's army, supported by the peasants, counter-attacked fiercely, and at the end of the five-day battle only a part of the Government's 5th Army was able to cut its way out, two divisions (those of Wang Chin-yü and Kung Ping-fan) losing much of their equipment and thousands of dead and wounded. The commands of Sun Lien-chung and Chi Hung-ch'ang suffered heavy losses. General Hu Tsu-yü (胡祖玉) was killed; Kung Ping-fan was wounded. The 19th Route Army, occupying a position

---

31. KUO MIN, May 18, 1931.

about 30 li from Chu Teh's base at Ningtu, in advance
of the flanking divisions, immediately after the
defeat of the 5th Army was ordered to withdraw to a
line continuous with other units on the right and left,
to strengthen the position of the Government's battle-
line. Before the manuever could be accomplished, Chu
Teh attacked with his main forces, broke the lines of
the 19th Army, then turned in a flanking movement and
defeated two divisions; he next turned back, defeated
the remainder of the 5th Army, and finally captured the
city of Nanfeng. Yungfeng and Taiho again fell into
the hands of the Reds. Chu Teh left Nanfeng and moved
rapidly east to the Fukien border, and there administered
a defeat to the 56th Division under Liu Ho-ting (   )
near Kienning, capturing two regiments; then the Reds
advanced rapidly down the Min River. On March 28, 1931,
an anti-Red expedition had left Swatow for an invasion
into the five hsien of western Fukien which the Communists
had controlled for about three years, returning with
considerable despatch on April 7th to report the re-
capture of Lungyen, Yungting, and Shanghang, and the
killing of 500 Reds. The Reds were in control of those
places in May, and subsequent to the defeat of Liu
Ho-ting captured Kienning, Taining, Chankuan, Shaowu,
and Chungan.[32]

The Government debacle marked the break-down of
their campaign. In the two weeks' fighting the Reds
were reported to have captured more than 20,000 rifles,

---

32. For a general account of the defeat, see especially
PEKING & TIENTSIN TIMES, June 11, June 16, 1931.

about 80 machine-guns, some trench-mortars and artillery,
and vast quantities of stores, and

> "With their fighting strength now greatly
> increased...the Communists are a formidable
> force, probably more than fifty percent
> stronger than when the campaign began against
> them, eight months ago."

The 19th Army withdrew to Kian, and the 6th, 11th,
and 14th Divisions were hurriedly moved from Hupeh
into the region south of Nanchang for the protection
of that city, communications between that city and
Kian having been cut. The 28th Division had been so
badly beaten that it was withdrawn to Hankow. In
Hupeh, about May 23rd, the 4th, 5th, and 15th Red
Armies had also counter-attacked, after their defeat
at Hsuanhuatien, and routed the regular forces at
Sungfu (near Macheng), capturing 500 troops with all
their equipment. The end of the second punitive
expedition, lasting about six months, had been reached.

In December 1930, the Red troops in the Fukien-
Kiangsi-Hunan area may have numbered, exlusive of large
numbers of Red Guards and Youth Guards et cetera, as
many as 62,000 fighting men, but very probably no more
than this. These were divided into Red Armies composed
of, ordinarily, 1-5,000 men, most of the Red troops
being stationed in the mountainous country that makes
up south-eastern Kiangsi and western Fukien, comprising
a solid block of territory extending from a line through
Nanfeng and Loan as far south as Hsinfeng and Anyuan,
bounded on the west by the Kan River, and on the east by
Lungyen and Kueihua in Fukien. Besides this area, the
region around Hsiushui and T'ungku was held by a force of
about 10,000 Reds, and Fang Chih-min and Shao Shih-p'ing

held control the north-eastern part of the province.

The most foolish of tacticians would not have
hurled 60,000 ill-equipped men against 200,000. The
decision to split the already small Red concentrations
into still smaller guerilla groups (which were, however,
readily amassed for heavy attacks) dissipated the force
of the Government's offensive in the mountains and woods
of the area. When they moved in sluggish heavy formations,
the Reds danced out of the way; when the Government
troops split up into smaller groups, the Reds combined
and struck. The Reds operated with the benefit of the
assistance of the population, besides being better
acquainted with the country in the first place. The
regular troops, strangers in a hostile territory where
the population (upon which they were billeted) remembered
them from times past, could not move with the sure
knowledge that they were not being led either many weary
miles astray or straight into a trap, airplanes being of
little value. The attempt to surround the whole of the
Red armies in an effort to finish up the job with one
blow proved impossible.

There were other reasons for the failure than the
fact that the Reds were desperate fighters. During the
period of the second campaign, there was a serious division
of responsibility in the province. Chu Shao-liang,
heading the 6th Route Army, had his regular station at
Nanfeng and should have been in control in that area.
Wang Chin-yü was Tupan for the Defence of the Hunan-Kiangsi
Border, stationed at Nanchang. Ho Ying-ch'in was head of
the anti-Red campaign, also stationed at Nanchang, as was

Chairman Lu Ti-p'ing, who had the political and military
responsibility in the province. But, for the whole
campaign, final responsibility rested in Nanking. There
was a complete lack of unity of command. The fighting
was characterized on the Government side by a lack of
relish for battle, there being evident the strong deisre
of every military organization that some other unit
bear the brunt of the Red blows. One indication of the
character of the Government attack may be discovered in
the KUO MIN account on June 29th of the circumstances of
a "victory" won by the Nanking troops (the defeat related
above):

> "The battle-field was strewn with killed and
> wounded outlaws. A number also met death by
> electrocution when they came into contact with
> electric barbed-wires which form part of the
> formidable defence works of the Government
> forces."

An important contributory factor in the defeat of
the Government was that, just as in 1930 when the Reds
made such important gains in strength, there was civil
war in China - at least in open prospect. The Kuangtung
declaration of independence of April 30th left the
country in a state of latent warfare, and no general in
Kiangsi knew when it would be necessary for him to turn
his front toward some other enemy for his own preservation.
Among the Government troops in Kiangsi there was also
considerable doubt as to what exactly was the attitude of
Ch'en Ming-shu's (陳 銘 樞) 19th Route Army, even up
until the end of the period of the campaign. The Canton
group were also stigmatized by the Government as "Reds",
cooperating with the Communists in Kiangsi in an attempt
to overthrow the Kuomintang and the State, just as like

imprecations had been hurled at various of the 1930
rebels. But the Nanking group would, nevertheless,
negotiate with the deluded for their return to the
fold. In its telegram of May 30th to the Central
Executive Committee (CEC) members in the Canton group,
the CEC of the Kuomintang charged that

> "Comrade Chiang Kai-shek has laboured day and
> night for the suppression of banditry. Just
> when his plans have been completed and
> extermination of banditry assured, your present
> associates are contemplating to lift the siege
> against banditry by creating trouble. If you
> do not awake immediately, the country will be
> deluged with the 'Red' flood and the race will
> be enslaved and the nation will face extinction.
> It will be a crime for which you will never be
> excused by the world and the spirit of our late
> Leader."

In the middle of June, Ch'en Ming-shu wired to Wang
Ching-wei explaining his attitude in part as follows:

> "The Red Evil in Kiangsi is terrible. If
> it is left unsuppressed, not only the Kuomintang
> but the State will be destroyed. Being urged by
> the Central Government authorities, and pricked
> by conscience, I found it impossible to remain
> passive, and have made up my mind to take part
> in military affairs, determined to do my best
> for the suppression of the Communist-bandits.
> I believe that questions relating to the Party
> should be left to it to be disposed of, and that
> for the present, we all should combine our efforts
> for the destruction of the Communists."[33]

Wang Ching-wei replied:

> "Those who are entrusted with the work of
> subjugating Communist-bandits should exert
> their utmost to carry out their duties with
> which they are entrusted. Chiang Kai-shek not
> only abandoned the work of suppressing them
> till recently, but now employs troops not
> directly under his command, to be made the
> target of by the Red Army, for the purpose of
> being destroyed by it. Accordingly, they are
> neither paid nor supplied with food. There is
> no word strong enough to condemn his cruelty.
> As long as Chiang Kai-shek remains at the head
> of the Government, the suppression of the
> Communists is impossible. Our Government has

---

33. RENGO, PEKING & TIENTSIN TIMES, June 19, 1931.

its own plan of subjugating them. And should
Chiang Kai-shek ever advance his troops into
Kwangtung, the cradle of the Revolution, under
the pretext of putting down the Communists,
our armed men will rise against him. We are
pleased to hear you to (sic) have made yourself
interested in military affairs again, and hope
that you will come back to Canton to assist us.
If, however, it is impossible for you to return
to Canton at once, you should support the
declaration made public by the extraordinary
meeting of the Central and Supervisory Committees
of the Kuomintang, in order to make the blood of
Chiang Kai-shek congeal with terror."[34]

This was hardly an atmosphere in which to expect
cooperative effort for the solution of the problems
confronting the nation.

With the Reds avoiding contact with the main
strength of the Government forces and winning most
of the battles (usually of their own seeking) with
detached Government units, their strength underwent
considerable increase during the period they were
being "exterminated". Concerning Government losses
no official figures were given out, but a newspaper
correspondent estimated that "the losses in the anti-
Red campaign have been no less than in the war with
Feng and Yen, counting deaths and desertions. So,
the troops have all been enlisting the peasants, and
others, to fill up their ransks."[35] The Government
losses in defeats, desertions, and in the sale of
munitions, sufficed to increase the Red armies by,
probably, about 20,000 men, giving them a total of
some 80,000 armed troops who were much richer in
equipment and experience than before. The Commanding

34. RENGO, PEKING & TIENTSIN TIMES, June 19, 1931.
35. TA KUNG PAO, July 12, 1931.

Officer of the Yangtze Patrol reported on June 25th

from Hankow that

> "The bandit-communist menace is increasing in
> the Southern part of Kiangsi Province. It is
> estimated that there are from 80,000 to 100,000
> armed bandits in the province who are being
> opposed by about 250,000 Nationalist troops.
> Recent reports indicate that in the engagements
> which have occured (sic) so far, the bandits
> have had the better of it."

4. Third Punitive Expedition (July-September 1931).

About the middle of June 1931, Chiang Kai-shih

himself arrived in Nanchang. He straightforth issued

orders that no intelligence concerning troop movements

and anti-Red activities should be permitted to leak out,

instituted strict censorship over post and telegraph

concerning such news, and directed besides, on June

28th, that mendacious reports of victories should cease

thenceforth. It was reported that he caused the

execution of eight regimental commanders for failure

to display proper energy in prosecution of the campaign,

and, during the month, about 100,000 more troops were

moved into the province. July 1st was set for the

beginning of the "final" offensive, and as the time

approached Chiang Kai-shih caused to be distributed to

the population by 'plane the following proclamation:

> "Generalissimo has personally come to save
> you. Privates in brigand armies who voluntarily
> come to the Revolutionary Army (that is, Chiang's
> - EC) will be well treated. Only the brigand
> leaders, Chu Teh and Mao Tse-tung, will be killed.
> Brigand soldiers will not be permitted to be
> killed. You poor inhabitants under coercion
> (sic), come quickly to join the Revolutionary
> Army. You people in the bandit-infected (sic)
> districts, rise up quickly and kill all the red
> brigands in order to regain your freedom. Red
> brigands are brutes which oppress both the soldiers
> and the people. Red brigands are fatherless and
> motherless brutes. Kill the leaders of the brigand

armies; come quickly to join the Revolutionary
Army. Surely you will be rewarded. Nobody
is permitted to kill or hurt the people.
Brigand soldiers, come quickly to join the
Revolutionary Army. Each brigand soldier who
comes with a rifle will be rewarded $30. Red
brigands are low and mean.[36]

The difficulties in logic experienced by the author of
the proclamation doubtless derived from the fact that
he was, at the same time, attempting to weedle the
"Red brigands" into coming forward to partake of
Nanking mercy the while he called upon the population
in which is rooted the Communist movement to rise up
and smite the "Red brigands" who are of them, so that
they could again enjoy the rule of the Kuomintang.
"Surely you will be rewarded", but the peasantry
have developed a Cartesian skepticism of Kuomintang
protestations these years.

In Fukien, after the fall of Kienning and Shaowu,
no programs of attack against the Reds were laid. The
general feeling seemed to be that if Foochow could be
saved that fact itself would be occasion for thankfulness.
The Reds held, roughly, the western half of the province,
the line running through Kienning, Shunchang, Yungan,
Lungyen, and Yungting. In Kiangsi, with the collapse
of the plan to surround the Reds, the Communist forces
had got back into pretty much their original positions
in the southern part of the province; Fang Chih-min and
K'ung Ho-ch'ung still were in north-east and north-west,
respectively. The Government decided to attack along
three routes; by the Left Route Army, under Ho Ying-ch'in
advancing from Nanfeng; by the Right Route Army, under

---

36. Lockhart, Hankow, July 3, 1931.

Ch'en Ming-shu, advancing from Kian; and the Central
Route Army under Sun Lien-chung, advancing from Loan.
The Government's line was thus Kian-Loan-Nanfeng -
and if the Reds fled into Kuangtung presumably Nanking
would not feel badly. There were about ten divisions
being divided fairly equally between the other two
fronts. The Red forces of Chu Teh, P'eng Teh-huai,
and Lo Ping-hui (羅 炳 輝) were concentrated in the
Juichin - Shihcheng area; Huang Kung-lueh and Li Ming-jui
(李 明 瑞) evidently were on the west bank of the Kan
River in the Yunghsin - Suichuan region. The base of
military supplies for the Government forces of the Left
and Central Routes was at Ihuang, some 120 li from the
nearest Government positions, through hard country. But
many coolies were being impressed in Honan, Hupeh, and
Kiangsi, and herded down to Kiangsi like cattle, except
for the chains. If they were not shot trying to escape,
or did not die of suffocation in the closed iron cars in
which they were transported, or did not die otherwise
of ill-treatment, they transported the supplies for
the Government army.[37]

But RENGO remarked at this time that,

> "with the exception of a very few divisions under
> direct command of the Nanking Government, remarkable
> lack of martial spirit is noted among officers and
> men at the front, to the great annoyance of those
> in supreme command."

In Hupeh, Ho Lung captured Fanghsien. In Hopei the
Provincial Government, finding at the beginning of July
that six months of effort had not sufficed for the

---

37. See KUO WEN report, Peiping, June 30, 1931, concerning
    petition of Honan Famine Relief Association to Chiang
    Kai-shih and Chairman Liu Chih asking that impressment
    of laborers for the Kiangsi expedition be stopped;
    also, CENTRAL CHINA POST, May 26, 1931; PEKING &
    TIENTSIN TIMES, July 1, 1931; Lockhart's political
    report, July 3, 1931, from Hankow.

extermination of the banditry in the province within the time limit, respectfully requested the Executive Yuan to extend the limit for three months more, "because of the special circumstances attending the task in Hopei"; permission was granted.[38]

The general offensive, scheduled for July 1, 1931, began about July 6th. The small cities in the path of the Nanking troops fell with no trouble, and Chu Shao-liang and Ch'en Ch'eng (陳　誠) (making up the Left Wing) preceeded east through Kangtu for an encircling movement around Kuangchang. Sun Lien-chung and Ch'en Ming-shu both advanced without effort toward Shachi for the attack on Ningtu. Chiang Kai-shih reported that Kuangchang was captured by Government troops on July 12th. According to other official reports, on July 16th there were taken Shihcheng and Kienning (Fukien), while Tungku fell on the 17th; Hsingkuo and Ningtu were being besieged, it was said, the latter by 80,000 troops; the Red troops on the Kiangsi-Fukien border were reported surrounded by Fukien armies. A glance at the map will give a better understanding of the apparent extent and vigor of the Government's operations. Thirteen thousand "war captives", peasants, were brought back from the front, to "assist in their reform". T. V. Soong sent a telegram to Chang Hsueh-liang stating that the anti-Red expedition was progressing successfully and would be ended shortly; "Replying Marshal Chang thanks Mr. Soong for his information, and requests him to give him a fuller report on the bandit suppression work."[39]

---

38. TA KUNG PAO, July 18, 1931.
    KUO WEN, July 14, 1931.
39. KUO WEN, July 14, 1931.

On July 19th the Government forces captured Ningtu "after the town had been literally bombed from the face of the earth"[40] ".....now, with the capture of Ningtu, only Tungku remains" (see above for previous report of capture of Tungku). Chiang Kai-shih on July 16th announced rewards of $50,000 each for Chu Teh, Mao Tse-tung, P'eng Teh-huai, and Huang Kung-lueh, alive; $20,000 would be given for the head of any of the four; but a liberal policy would be adopted by the conquering armies toward the population: "The order forbids the ruthless and indiscriminate slaughter of the ignorant peasant followers and urges that only the leaders be killed."[41]

On July 25th, the Reds abandoned Tungku and it was really entered by the Government troops; as the Nanchang correspondent of the NORTH CHINA HERALD wrote, "Tung-ku for the first time is really captured by the government force". The troops consummated their victory by burning the premises of the Peasants and Laborers Bank. Important captures of munitions were reported, together with heavy losses on the part of the Red forces, and "General Ho Ying-ch'in reports that a death-blow has been dealt to the Reds by the recent victories of the Government."[42]

As usual, the Government reports turned out to be somewhat exaggerated. The Reds had retreated before the on-coming Government forces, but with only minor losses; the bombing of Ningtu was real enough, but it was the

40. The reports stated that no less than 120 bombs weighing 150 pounds each were dropped; see also TA KUNG PAO of November 7, 1931, for account of bombing of innocent villages in south-eastern Honan under the impression they were "Red".
41. KUO MIN, July 16, 1931.
42. KUO MIN, July 20, 1931.

population that suffered chiefly from the action, and not the Communists. The Red armies retired to the region around Hsingkuo, Huichang, Yütu, and Juichin, and the conflict entered its final phases. Hsingkuo and Yütu were reported besieged by the Nanking forces, while the rest of the Reds were being "hotly pursued". On July 31st, exactly according to the program, the following news item was sent out from Nanking by REUTER:

> "General Chiang Kai-shek has officially reported to the Government the capture of all the Communist strong-holds in Kiangsi and states that the Government campaign against the Communists has been successfully completed."

Although the issuing of this statement was doubtless in large part motivated by a desire to follow the time schedule that had been decided upon, the declaration of victory was also probably made with an eye on Shih Yu-san's "Little War", which seemed to have in it elements of coalition against Chiang which would cause him to throw his harried energies in yet another direction. Chiang left Nanchang for Nanking on July 18th, returning on the 28th.

The capture of Hsingkuo was announced on August 4th; Huang Kung-lueh and P'eng Teh-huai were reported as having been killed in action. Ts'ai T'ing-k'ai reported that Juichin was captured on the 7th, and the Reds in the Hsiushui-T'ungku region were said to have been suppressed. The National Government sent a telegram of congratulation to Chiang Kai-shih, concluding,

> "Jubilation mingled with a sense of relief is felt in learning the tidings of your success (over the Reds - EC). Please take good care of your health while discharging your arduous duties in the army.[43]

43. KUO MIN, August 7, 1931.

Thus commended,

> "Commander-in-Chief Chiang Kai-shek, in a circular
> order to the various military units participating
> in the present bandit-suppression campaign in
> Kiangsi, instructs that all remnant outlaws in
> the various recently captured districts must be
> rounded up within five days and that the 'Red'
> banditry in the whole province must be completely
> eradicated before the end of the current month so
> that the people may resume their occupations."[44]

Handbills were distributed by 'planes in Kiangsi,
directing the people to return to their homes within
three days and resume their occupations (the practice
of the Red population was to withdraw before the
advancing Government armies, taking with them all food
and fuel stores, and other supplies, leaving only a
bare land for the incoming troops).

The 11th, 12th, and 13th Red Armies took Yingshan
(Anhui) on August 1, 1931, disarming the 1,500 troops,
fully equipped with rifles and 18 machine-guns, and
killing the magistrate and Tangpu commissioner. In
Kiangsi, the Red armies counter-attacked fiercely.
Lungkang, Tungku, and Ningtu, were re-taken; the
divisions under Chao Kuan-t'ao and Ho Meng-ling (郝夢齡)
were badly cut up in the fighting that took place in the
Huangpei-Hsiaopu and Lungkang and Liangtsun regions.
Chiang Kai-shih after his report of the completion of
the campaign had returned to Nanking, where he was
awaiting the return of T. V. Soong.

> "But in view of the critical situation at the front,
> resulted (sic) from the efforts of the Red remnants
> (their designation after July 31st - EC) in Kiangsi
> to start a counterattack to break through the cordon
> of the Government troops, he is forced to leave at
> once before Mr. Soony's return to take personal
> command and bring the anti-Red expedition to a speedy
> end at an early date."[45]

---

44. ASIATIC, August 16, 1931.
45. ASIATIC, August 22, 1931.

At the weekly Memorial Service at Nanchang on
August 25th, Chiang called upon the Bandit-Suppression
Forces to exert themselves "in the last five minutes"
to wipe out the vestiges of banditry in Kiangsi before
the convocation of the Congress of the Kuomintang on
October 10th. It was reported that,

> "With the return of the Commander-in-Chief, the
> morale of the Government forces has increased.
> Consequently, marked progress has been made in
> the last few days. The 'Reds' fully aware of
> the Government's strong determination to
> eradicate banditry, are terror-stricken and
> are escaping in all directions... The fall of
> Juichin is expected shortly."[46]

Chiang Ting-wen stated that "the Government forces
have the bandits completely cut off. Their surrender
is imminent."[47] Chu Teh was said to be badly wounded,
with two foreign doctors in attendance; the Reds were
stated to be short of supplies, and therefore dying
"by the hundreds" of starvation.

> "General Chao Kuan-t'ao reports to the local
> Headquarters saying that within half a month
> most of the Communist-bandits will be starved
> to death. General Chao adds that the Red
> troops are suffering from epidemic diseases.
> Military reports declare that the Communist-
> bandits will not be able to break through the
> cordons of mines planted by the government
> forces. The government troops have entrenched
> themselves behind the mines. The largest Red
> forces remaining are said to be holding the
> mountain fastnesses at Hsinkuo (Hsingkuo - EC).
> They number several thousand strong."[48]

On August 29th, Li Ming-jui launched a heavy attack on
Kanchow, but was beaten back by the garrison. In Hupeh,
Hsu Yuan-ch'üan's troops operated successfully east of
the River, driving K'uang Chi-hsun east into Anhui and
north. KUO WEN on September 8th again announced the

---

46. KUO MIN, August 27, 1931.
47. KUO MIN, August 28, 1931.
48. KUO WEN, September 4, 1931.

capture of Juichin, with the capture of 600 Reds.

On September 7th to 9th, the biggest battle of the campaign was fought at Kaohsing, the 19th Route Army constituting the strength of the Government force. Of the Red remnants, according to the report of Ch'en Ming-shu, 50,000 troops participated, of whom, he continued, over 10,000 were killed, while 1,000 rifles were captured. He continued,

> "From the time our armies surrounded the bandits up to the present, this is the first time we ever came to grips with them in battle. The ferocity of the bandits and the way they die is startling, and this was such a battle as is rarely seen; the bandits, having suffered this severe blow, surely cannot move again."[49]

Chiang Kai-shih reported the battle at the current Nanking Memorial Service, stating that all the Red haunts in Kiangsi had been destroyed, with many Soviet officials captured "and dealt with according to law"; over 22,000 Reds were killed in the battle, he declared, and P'eng Teh-huai had been badly wounded; "The Red bandits having suffered this bitter blow certainly cannot rise up again, and the whole lot can soon be wiped out."[50] The invasion of Hunan from Kuangsi threatened, and the 19th Route Army proceeded to Kanchow; other units were withdrawn from the Kiangsi front for service in Hunan on the Hengchow front. The Nanking Government again charged that the Liangkuang (Kuangtung-Kuangsi) were acting in collusion with the Reds, assisting them with their flanking attack and supplying them with munitions.[51]

---

49. TA KUNG PAO, September 15, 1931.
50. ibid.
51. TA KUNG PAO, September 13, 1931.

It seems evident that both the 19th Army and the
Red troops suffered heavy losses at Kaohsing, although
no decisive victory was won by either. Moreover, it
may be that Huang Kung-lueh was killed, really, in this
battle, and his troops badly cut up. But it marked the
end of the campaign, for, what with the heart-breaking
conditions under which the troops had to operate in
Kiangsi, and the combination of the Liangkuang threat
and the emergence of the Sino-Japanese conflict on
September 18th, Nanking had had a surfeit of exterminating
the Reds, who, at the end of the drive, were concentrated
in the districts of Juichin, Huichang, Yütu, and Kanchow.

It was, however, necessary to minimize the
significance of the withdrawal from the battle-field
in Kiangsi. On September 28th ASIATIC reported that
Chu Teh and Mao Tse-tung had offered to surrender to the
Nanking Government so that they could lead their forces
to the front against the Japanese. On the 30th, Nanking
stated that Hsiung Shih-hui (熊式輝) had arrived at
Nanchang from the anti-Red front, presumably for the
purpose of discussing the surrender of the prominent
Reds, "who have offered their services to lead their
forces to Manchuria to evict the Japanese usurper".
The Nanchang staff of the Generalissimo Headquarters
returned to Nanking about October 1st, and the military
action against the Reds was ended.

The Pacific Institute, meeting in Shanghai about
this time, reached certain comforting conclusions:

> "Communism in China is a doctrine entirely foreign
> to the genuine nature and antecedents of the
> people, and, even in the districts where Bolshevism

reigns to-day, it is practiced in a manner wholly at variance with the orthodox tenets of Lenin, according to conclusions arrived at yesterday by delegates to the Institute of Pacific Relations Conference...."[52]

It is notorious that the Chinese leaders, in their propaganda, indulge themselves in the matter of wish-thinking. Particularly as regards Communism, this attitude was well exemplified by a pronounciamento of Dr. Tchou Ngao-hsiang, Director for Foreign Affairs of the ephemeral Feng-Yen-Wang Peiping Government of 1930, who stated in August of that year that the Soviet system is wholly unsuited to China, because:

"(1) Chinese farmers unlike the Russian peasants are also land-owners, though their holdings being (sic) small.
"(2) Chinese land-owners are extremely lenient with their employees in sharing their yearly crops.
"(3) Chinese farmers are the most law-abiding elements of the population and condemn anything like murder and incendiarism, both individually and collectively.
"(4) Chinese farmers have a very deep sense of honor and all entertain high hopes in being able to acquire their land-holdings through their daily toil and by means of their hard savings."

The hot pursuit of this particular ignis fatuus would probably prove completely disastrous.

But, of Kiangsi it was written from Kiukiang that the

"Communists are again re-occupying districts and cities, and increasing the area of their control. The ill-behaviour of not a few of the regular troops, and their oppression of the common people, has led to these Communists being welcomed back by the mass of the population in some parts, though the wealthy have had to flee or go into hiding, or suffer capture or death."[53]

In the Tehsing and Loping area of north-eastern Kiangsi, the Reds came back in full strength, and in Hunan, Hupeh,

---

52. PEKING & TIENTSIN TIMES, October 29, 1931; the Institute's authorities on Leninism were not designated.
53. PEKING & TIENTSIN TIMES, October 30, 1931.

Honan, and Anhui, the activities of the Red armies
increased in extent and vigor. Ho Lung captured
Anlu on October 14th, and he and Tuan Teh-ch'ang
took in rapid succession Paichow, Hsinkow, Chunghsiang, and Yochiakow. Along the Hunan-Kiangsi border,
by November 1st, four Red units were established in
the following areas: T'ungku-Hsiushui, Pinghsiang-
Lienhua, Chaling-Yuhsien, and Pingkiang-Liuyang.
On November 7, 1931, the Second All-China Conference
of Soviets met and established the Provisional
Government of the Chinese Soviet Republic (PGCSR) at
Juichin, Kiangsi.

From that time until the present the Communist
movement has suffered but small hinderance from the
side of law and order. With the crushing misery of
the people aggravated still further by the ravages of
the flood, the popular protest continues to swell in
the heart of agrarian China. At the time of the
establishment of the PGCSR, it was noted in that
connection by a Hankow paper that:

> "in reality it is a very tragic business. From
> whatever angle one views such a situation one
> cannot avoid the conclusion that an unhappy people
> have been driven to the verge of desperation by
> unmitigated repression and rapacity where they
> expected, and were fully entitled to, something
> far different. It was not armies that brought
> Canton from the South to the North, but the
> hospitality of a people weary of oppression and
> hopeful that the promises of better days would be,
> at least in part, implemented by those who made
> them as soon as the ruling power became theirs....
> Never before had an invading army been welcomed
> by the people and their reward has been that
> whereas their former masters beat them with whips,
> since getting rid of them they have had a taste
> of scorpions. The breaking point must be reached
> sooner or later and every sign now points to that
> point being about reached. It is only a month or
> two since Nanking's claim to have completely

eliminated communist influence from Kiangsi was
broadcasted to the world. That the claim and
campaign alike were fraudulent is now being
proved, but only after the Western world has
accepted Nanking statements at their face value
and thus helped to give a new lease of life to
those mainly responsible for the present
situation, not only in Kiangsi but all over
China and Manchuria. If a Soviet Republic (sic)
ever becomes a fact, it will be due more to its
opponents in the National Government than it
will be to the ability or efforts of its
supporters either from Soviet Russia or the left
wing of the Kuomintang in China. This latter
might have been directed into constructive
channels and unity ultimately achieved, but it has
been sacrificed to expediency and selfishness."[54]

In the latter part of December 1931, REUTER reported
that, far from the Reds being exterminated, the authorities
were considerably exercised by the threat of a march on
Nanchang by the "Red remnants"; in Hupeh, continued the
account, 60 out of a total of 70 hsien were in the hands
of the Communists; while at Ningtu (?) nine regiments
of Sun Lien-chung's ex-Kuominchün troops, considered
some of the best regular troops operating in the campaign,
had turned over to the Reds because they had been without
pay for five months and were without provender.[55] These
troops occupied Tingchow in Fukien, and at present
(in April) are threatening Amoy.

In Fukien the peasants, oppressed beyond endurance
by the vicious soldiery, in the latter part of December
gathered to the sound of gongs beaten from the hill-tops
and wiped out more than one-half the regular troops
stationed in that area.

"This is the first time we have known of a populace
arising in mass against the military, looked upon
as a common foe. Village feuds have for the time
been buried and, side by side, these villagers have
pressed forward unfalteringly against a well-trained
army. There has been nothing savouring of radicalism

54. CENTRAL CHINA POST, November 25, 1931.
55. PEKING & TIENTSIN TIMES, December 31, 1931.

or communism in this movement, nor has there
been any disorder as the farmer army has pressed
its foe back from village to village."[56]
As regards the relations of the troops with
the peasant population, it is interesting to
note the five regulations issued by Chiang
Ting-wen in September (?) 1931 for the control
of his unit: "those committing rape shall be
shot; those stealing the people's goods shall
be shot; those using force in the purchase or
sale of things shall be shot; those injuring
the people shall be shot; those forcibly taking
the people's livestock shall be shot." This is
reminiscent of Liu Hsiang's famous seven-word
order on how to clear the Szechuan countryside
of troublesome elements: "Sha (殺 kill - EC)!
Sha! Sha! Sha! Sha! Sha! Sha!"

In Hupeh, there are about 200,000 regular troops.
In December 1931, Huangan was taken by the Reds, the
69th Division being almost annihilated and its
commander, Chao Kuan-yin (趙 冠 英), killed. At
the same time, there was a movement by the Reds under
Tuan Teh-ch'ang and K'ung Ho-ch'ung, stationed on
opposite sides of the Yangtze, to establish contact
between their forces in the region of Pailochi for
the apparent purpose of extending the Red control to
several more towns along the river in that area. After
cutting up the 69th at Huangan, the Reds under K'uang
Chi-hsun crowded down on Huangpei, 20 miles north of
Hankow, at the same time other Red troops came up from
the south. Foreign missionaries evacuated into Hankow
from Shekow, 10 miles to the north; from the south, the
Reds came so close that the Catholic missions in Hanyang,
across the river from Hankow, evacuated into the latter
place, from where the sounds of machine-gun and rifle-
fire were distinctly audible. On January 27th, 2,000
Red troops under Ho Ying (Ho Lung's eldest sister) and

---

56. PEKING & TIENTSIN TIMES, January 2, 1932.

captured Fianglingchi on the river near Hanyang. The
pressure on the Wuhan cities was later released, but
there has been heavy fighting during most of the month
of April between the Reds under Tuan Teh-ch'ang and
Ho Lung, and several of Hsu Yuan-ch'üan's 10th Army
units - the 41st, 44th, and 48th Divisions, and two
other brigades - in the region of Tienmen, Tsaoshih,
and Yingcheng. There have been heavy losses on both
sides, and it is evident that there has been no
decisive victory gained one way or the other.

The situation in Honan, where the many civil
wars that have trampled down its fields have left the
countryside in deepest poverty, and with the gift of
a wealth of banditry for their scourge, one bit more was
added to the people's burden when some of Sun Tien-ying's
(孫殿英) troops, long unpaid, burst out of Shansi
into Honan and lost themselves in the roving bands that
kill and rob mercilessly (largely because all other
means of livelihood have been cut off) From Huangchuan
in the southern part of the province a correspondent
wrote under date of January 28, 1932, that:

> "Last August, this district was invaded by a
> band of reds, numbering more than 10,000 (ten
> thousand). They robbed everything they could put
> their hands on, but refrained from killing and
> burning. After they left; a division of government
> soldiers took possession of the district town and
> behaved themselves far worse than the reds. The
> people said of them that they practized (sic) all
> the four characters 'Chien, lou, shao, sha' (to rape,
> to rob, to burn, to kill). And what did they not
> not do to foreign property? The reds took away
> only personal effects; but the so called regular
> soldiers burned down everything; furniture, doors,
> windows and ceilings. I could do nothing to stop
> .em, because too far away from foreign gunboats."[57]

---

57. CENTRAL CHINA POST, January 1, 1932; see also TA KUNG
    PAO, November 7, 1931, referring to the Reds in Honan,
    f the belief that "The garrison troops' actions are
    no different from those of bandits."

It has recently been remarked that in Honan, because
of the galling suffering the population is experiencing
in its indescribable poverty, the people are turning in
their desperation to Communism, and "if fundamental
assistance is not given quickly it is to be feared that
the whole province will become a second Kiangsi."[58] On
March 3rd, Rev./Heier wrote from the Catholic Mission
at Huangchuan:

> "Anent our communistic troubles - well, the
> Reds are at our doors. Sometimes we flee from
> the city - then we come back again. A constant
> state of uncertainty.
>
> "Beginning February there was one serious
> attack on the city, after which things quieted
> down again. Right now it is Kushih, a city
> some forty miles east that's seriously threatened.
> Shangcheng fell into the hands of the Reds about
> a month ago. For about a month and a half the
> Reds have been hammering hard along the entire
> front here, and with no small success. The
> Government armies haven't won a single fight yet -
> and no one knows how many guns and machine guns
> have been literally thrown at the communists. In
> fact the whole Government resistance has been
> nothing but a joke. - I say 'resistance' because
> the Reds are plainly on the offensive.
>
> "The whole trouble lies in the fact that the
> common soldier doesn't fight. Without pay for
> half a year and some. The soldiers are just mad. -
> and what's worse. They are not even being fed now
> - and clothed only raggedly. For the past few weeks
> these three divisions here have been subsisting on
> what everybody got for himself - the praedatory (sic)
> system! And, of course the public groans, and gets
> more and more convinced that the Reds might be a
> blessing to this country after all. The army General,
> Chang-fang, came over from Sinyang a few days ago
> and has taken up quarters here in the city, whether
> things will get much better now remains to be seen.
> One thing seems to be certain, unless these soldiers
> here are well paid and well fed, the Reds will carry
> the day, and that before the next crop is in."

On April 7, 1932, he wrote again to report that the
anti-Red campaign, which had been in progress for about

58. TA KUNG PAO, February 5, 1932.

a month, was having "no more than about a fifty-fifty success".

> "Old Chang Fang (the Nanking general in charge of the campaign - EC) is anxious to make a success of the task entrusted to him, so he is baiting his troops on in every possible way he can. The latest incentive is a promise of a week's free rampage in and around the city of Shangcheng - if retaken. I know of two particular cases within the past two years where a similar promise spelled victory. It puts a new kind of spirit into the men altogether. The men fight - and they get there. Of course I wouldn't care to be in Shangcheng during that week's 'celebration'. When Shangcheng is retaken there'll be a great victory reported to Headquarters, and the Government will be happy - but not the people of Shangcheng. But then in these Chinese wars it's after all the public that be damned."

The latest military tactics of the Government in their struggle with the Reds contemplate the division of the several provinces up into sections, in each of which certain troops shall have the responsibility for cleaning up the territory. At the same time, there are to be organized groups of militia locally, for self-defence against the Reds. Hupeh has been divided into five sections, and the responsibility allotted; Hunan has eight divisions; in Honan, where the Reds are concentrated in a comparatively small area, Chang Fang is leading a drive against the Communist region. With the advance of Sun Lien-chung's troops on Amoy, the Fukien authorities are doubtless too busy taking defensive measures to spend much time drawing up schemes for exterminating the Reds. It is, of course, Kiangsi that holds the center of the stage at the present time, so far as Communism is concerned. From the beginning of the year until the first of March, the Reds had extended their territory by six hsien in the southern part of the province, and Kanchow was besieged by P'eng Teh-huai for about a month, from February 4th until March 1st, before the Government's relief of three divisions arrived to aid the lone brigade under Ma K'un (馬 崑) that was holding the city; it was only the excellent strategic position of the place that saved it from capture. On April 6th, KUO WEN reported from Nanchang that the Central Government had issued an order setting a time-limit of three months for the final suppression of the Reds in Kiangsi, and that Kiangsi, Hunan, Hupeh, Fukien, and Kuangtung troops would cooperate in the task, all of them to be under the direction of Ch'en Chi-t'ang, with the assistance of Chu Shao-liang.[59] Ch'en Chi-t'ang's concentration in northern Kiangsi had begun in the latter part of February, before the issue of this order and before he had been promised $2,000,000 per month for military expenses to be incurred in connection with the drive against the Communists by two routes - into Fukien and into Kiangsi. And, on April 19th, the National Government issued a mandate appointing Ho Ying-ch'in Commander for the Suppression of Brigandage on the Kiangsi-Kuangtung-Fukien Borders, with Ch'en Chi-t'ang Vice-Commander.[60]

Chu Teh and Lo Ping-hui are in western Fukien with their troops; Li Ming-jui, P'eng Teh-huai, and Huang Kung-lueh (?) are in the Juichin region. Fang Chih-min and K'ung Ho-ch'ung are still in the north-eastern and north-western sections of the province respectively.

---

59. TA KUNG PAO, April 8, 1932.
60. WUHAN JIH PAO, April 20, 1932.

There are 22 Government divisions listed for the task
of extermination - approximately 220,000 men if full
strength; and of these troops about 30,000 are Ch'en
Chi-t'ang's. There have already been reported
important victories for the Government; Li Ming-jui
is said to have been again killed. But this is all
of little importance, in the final analysis. Whether
it is probable that this expedition will be any more
successful than the three previous ones in accomplishing
the eradication of Communism from Kiangsi would seem to
depend upon two things - whether the various militarists
can maintain a unified front in China, and whether
anything will be done to better the conditions that make
for revolt. Melodious phrases alone will not suffice to
cement the Kuomintang together in strong unity, and -
were there that unity - Kuomintang promises would not be
enough to divert the peasantry of central China from
their jacquerie. Their miserable lot has only worsened
under the present regime, and they are rising in armed
protest.

The regular troops come from the soil originally,
and the senseless civil wars which they have waged,
knowing that they fought for nothing at all of any value,
have left them with the spirit of mercenaries who feel
that they have nothing to win by bravery, not even glory.
At the present time, with the meagre wages of most troops
far in arrears, they have no stomach for fighting the
peasantry. The Red armies now number at least 120,000
troops in central China, probably about equally distributed
north and south of the Yangtze; besides these, there are

the Red Guards, and other peasant organizations that
are firm in their support of the Red military
organization. All these are prepared to fight
desperately because they feel that they have nothing
to lose. Their organization is close-knit and
disciplined, and they look toward convincing the
peasantry, laboring class, and soldiery of China
that they would be better off fighting under the Red
banner. One ought out to be surprised, in such
circumstances, if the fourth punitive expedition
leaves China as badly off as before.

III. THE CHINESE SOVIETS

1. Locus.

Apart from the few days'control of Nanchang in
1927, the Soviet Power first made its appearance in
Kiangsi in the Spring of 1928, when Chu Teh established
a soviet at Chingkangshan. The four years that have
elapsed since then have sufficed for the growth of a
movement which has established firm control over a
large section of the Kiangsi-Fukien region, as well as
important areas in the Yangtze valley. Juichin, the
capital of the Soviet Government, is located nearly in
the center of the Soviet area, which is very mountainous.
The boundaries of the region under the Red influence
can be traced, roughly, through Kuangchang (Kiangsi),
Kueihua (Fukien), Changping (Fukien), Tapu (Kuangtung),
Anyuan (Kiangsi), Kanchow, and Kian. Besides the
Soviet Government of China, there are provincial
governments, two of which fall within the limits of the
area of which Juichin is the center. Tungku is said to

be the provincial capital for Kiangsi, and Tingchow
(formerly Lungyen) is the seat of the Minsi (閩　西 -
Western Fukien) Soviet Government. The Red forces of
the whole area are available for the defence of any
part, which would give an effective army of about
40,000; if Sun Lien-chung's rebellious troops can be
counted as Reds - and, at the least, they wear Red
arm-bands, are hostile toward the constituted authorities,
and are claimed by the Reds as their own - the Red armies
there can then be numbered at 60,000 fighters.

South of this region, in eastern Kuangtung, there
is a Soviet area which has persisted since 1930. Its
area is bounded on the south by Kaifeng and Lufeng
(where Ho Lung and Yeh T'ing were active in the first
six months of 1928), and includes the mountainous
territory directly north as far as Tzechin and Shuichai.
So far as is known, this organization is largely under
the control of the peasants themselves, with comparatively
little military force, and is apparently but little
molested by the Kuangtung authorities.

The third Soviet region centers about Lienhua,
Kiangsi, and is demarcated by the points Anfu, Yunghsin,
Suichuan, and Chaling (Hunan). This is the area
ordinarily held by the army under Li Ming-jui, numbering
probably 5,000 troops.

Directly north is the T'ungku-Hsiushui Soviet region,
with the central organization reported to be located at
Chachin (Kiangsi). The outermost limits of its power
extend to Tayeh (Hupeh), Wuning (Kiangsi), Kaotsun
(Kiangsi, Wantsai hsien), Chiayi (Hunan), and Puchi (Hupeh).

K'ung Ho-ch'ung's Red Army is the military organization
for the area, with about 10,000 men.

In north-eastern Kiangsi is the Soviet with its
center probably somewhere in Tehsing hsien. Its area
is bordered by a line running through Wuyuan (Anhui),
Yüshan (Kiangsi), Chungan (Fukien), Yükiang (Kiangsi),
and Tehsing. The Red military forces here, numbering
some 5,000 troops, are under Fang Chih-min and his
lieutenant Shao Shih-p'ing.

The famous Hung Hu (洪 湖 - Big Lake), Hupeh,
Reds control the area bounded by Tsaoshih, Chujushan,
Pailochi, Kienli, and Tienmen, with the Soviet located
somewhere in Kienli hsien (in the region of Choulaotsui,
or Chuho?). The designation of this organization is:
"Kienli Hsien Soviet Government (監利縣蘇維埃政府)",
with control residing in a presidium. The Red troops
fighting in this region are those of Ho Lung and his
lieutenant Tuan Teh-ch'ang, and comprise about 15,000
troops. Many of these troops are not Hupeh men at all,
but remnants of the Kuangsi troops of Li Tsung-jen
and Hu Tsung-to 胡 宗 鐸), stranded there in 1929.

In the north-central part of Hupeh, the region
bordered by Tsaoyang, Suihsien, Chunghsiang, and Icheng
has been under the control of a Soviet for over three
years, with little molestation. Lushan and Paofeng are
the chief centers, and control is held by Chang Hsiang-
shan (張 香 山), but it is not known whether in a
military or political capacity. The group is under the
general control of Ho Lung, and has adopted a very
conciliatory policy toward the local peasantry, but
the passage of all mail and freight traffic over the

Fanchong-Kuangshui highway is on the sufferance of
the Red troops, unless accompanied by regular army
units. The military strength of this area is not
known, but it is probably less than 5,000 troops.

The Honan-Anhui-Hupeh Border Soviet Government
is the most important Communist political organization
north of the Yangtze. Its existence dates back
practically to the spring of 1928 when the struggle
in the cities was abandoned by the CCP and the members
of that Party went back to the villages to recuperate
their strength. The region includes some very rough
terrain, but is not so mountainous as that occupied by
the Reds in southern Kiangsi; the outer limits of its
territory are delimited by a boundary line running
through Huangchuan (Honan), Huochiu (Anhui), Liuan
(Anhui), Yingshan (Anhui), Huangkang (Hupeh), Yentzukang
(Huangpei hsien, Hupeh), and Kikungshan (Honan). The
Soviet Government for the region was established in
its present form in December 1929, with the capture of
Shangcheng, the leader at that time being Chow Wei-chiung
(周 維 烔). At any rate until recently, Cheng Hsing-wei
has been the Chairman of this Soviet Government, but it
has lately been reported that agents of Chiang Kai-shih,
presumably using the methods of bribery, had nearly
completed the corruption of a considerable section of
the leadership when the plot was discovered by Kuang
Chi-hsun and the guilty leaders killed. The result was
said to be a complete turn-over of control within the
organization, so that there is no certainty at present
concerning the personnel of the governing group. The

capital of the organization has been a shifting one,
having been at various times at Chiliping (Hupeh),
Chishihorhlientang (Hupeh), and Yenchiaho (Honan).
This area is strong in military strength, having at
least 30,000 troops, besides connections with (and
perhaps some military control from) K'uang Chi-hsun
with his army of some 10,000 men.

Control in these several areas is neither complete
nor irrevocable. In the border regions, clashes between
the regular troops and the Reds are frequent when either
the one or the other seeks to extend its influence. And,
upon the occasion of a concentration of the Government's
strength against the Communist region, the regulars, if
their strength is formidable at all, can go through the
Red area like a hot knife through butter, with the Reds
vanishing before them. To march through such a region,
however, is not to complete the conquest, and usually
the only part of such a country (where the population
as well as the opposing army is hostile) which can be
garrisoned is the hsien city. In the countryside, the
troops find great difficulty in getting supplies of food,
and only leave the walled cities on expeditions after
the elusive guerilla bands.

Oppositely, it is also true that the Red control
can be extended beyond the boundaries of the Soviet
regions with enough effectiveness to make raids on
trading centers for money and supplies. And, wherever
the Red armies travel the seeds of Communism are scattered,
so that there is always a harvest in prospect. K'uang
Chi-hsun, for one, roves at times through all that part
of Hupeh north of the Yangtze and east of the Ping-Han
Railway; the local soviets established under his influence

in eastern Hupeh were apparently wiped out in 1931 by the
10th Army under Hsu Yuan-ch'üan, but there is no reason
to believe the people have forgotten the principles they
were taught any more than they have the visiting wrath of
the "eradication". After Ho Lung left the Haofeng-Enshih
region in south-western Hupeh with his main military
strength, a part of his soviet organization collapsed, but
to compensate he ravaged the whole western part of the
province, the while his Political Officer, one Liu (劉),
spread doctrines of Sovietism among the peasantry. In
north-western Hupeh, where the Government's orders hardly
reach, there is little Communism and much of old-fashioned
banditry, with many Big Sword and Red Spear groups, but it
is probable that Ho Lung's drive into that area will not be
without its effects in the future. In Honan, too, where the
ubiquitous bandits would seem to deny the right of government
to either the Kuomintang or the Communists, there is nevertheless the beginning of the spread of Communist organization
from the east and south[61] into the south-central part of the

61. Bandit groups are frequently incorporated into Red armies
    although the settled policy of the CCP is that they shall
    not operate as a separate unit, but they shall be amalg-
    amated after they have undergone a purging of their former
    habits. With success, the bandit leader by the ordinary
    process of evolution becomes an aspirant to political
    power. When the notorious Widow Chang (張寡婦) was
    captured in Honan in 1931, before her execution she
    related the details of a conference that had been held in
    the spring of that year between various bandit leaders
    with the view of consolidating their forces into a
    political army. In Honan at the present time, certain
    bandits such as Ts'ui Erh-tan (崔二旦), Han Yü-ming
    (韓欲明), and Chang Kuo-jung (張國榮) might conceivably
    adhere to some political organization just as Fan Chung-
    hsiu became a political factor several years ago. In
    Suiyuan, Su Yü-sheng (蘇雨生) and Wang Ying (王英) have
    certain political characteristics, in southern Anhui Su
    Ming-chao (蘇明昭) leads the "First Heavenly Army (天下第一軍)",
    and in general it may be said that many peasant groups are
    embryo political groups. The story of Chang Tso-lin, of
    course, carries strong relevancy for the question of the
    potential evolution of bandit leaders.

province. In Hunan, where T'ang Sheng-chih with his sword first swept the country apparently clean of the popular organizations, and where no Red growths are visible today, it is said that the countryside is still honey-combed with Red cells. If this is true, the return of the Red strength into that province only waits upon some throw of the dice with which the national leaders gamble. Besides, there is Communist organization in the agrarian population in southern Kuangsi, east-central Kiangsu, in Shansi, and in western Chekiang. Economic distress and new political doctrine combine for the formation of a social revolution, and in China the one is increasing in severity and the other becoming more widespread. According to the Russian writer Mif,

> "The power of the soviets is spread in parts of the province of Kiangsi, and in important parts of Honan, Anhui, Hunan, Hupeh, and Fukien. Soviet shelters are discovered also in Kuangsi, Shansi, Shensi, and Szechuan. Approximately 1/6 of the territory of China proper (not counting the frontier territory) is seized now by the soviet movement."[62] This generalization, if it includes that territory where the struggle for power is now proceeding between the Red soviets and armies, and the regular authorities and their troops, is very nearly correct.

2. Soviet Action.

The practice of a Red Army when it captures a place is fairly uniform, varying only according to whether or not it is proposed to consolidate the Red power there. If it is a mere raid, the primary purpose is obviously the capture of money and supplies, and in furtherance of that design banks and public buildings are looted and demands for money made upon the rich persons of the place (often through the medium of the local Chamber of Commerce)

---

62. THE REVOLUTIONARY FIGHT IN CHINA, PRAVDA, November 12, 1931.

Besides, there are killed without mercy certain "enemies of the people". For instance, in the capture of Kuangshan, Honan, in October 1928, there were some 20 men especially stigmatized as "local tyrants" (土 豪), "evil gentry" (劣 紳), "greedy officials" (貪 官), and "lewd officers" (污 吏), and killed in the especially cruel fashions reserved for such categories. Among them were included the district magistrate, two Tangpu officials, an officer in a local society, the head of the Police Bureau and the head of the Tax Bureau.

There are destroyed all title deeds, records of indebtedness, et cetera, so as to release the poor from their obligations and wipe out so far as possible all evidence of the legal claim of the rich to a privileged economic status. Mass meetings are called, a few speeches made, and propaganda distributed. Replacements may be recruited for the ranks from among the villagers and armed with the equipment taken from the local militia. If it is harvest time and the Reds are in need of grain, a "Basket Brigade (籮 筐 隊)" will reap the fields before the troops pass on.[63]

However, if the Soviets are extending their territory, entry into the new area is under the recognized necessity, in the first place, of gaining the support of the population. At the same time, the Communist program demands a radical reorganization of the fundamental bases of the social system. The Reds are favored in their campaign because the vested interests are few in number, while the poorer class, who are promised better conditions, is in the great majority.

---

63. TA KUNG PAO, November 6, November 8, 1931.

When a Red Army comes in under such circumstances, every
effort is made from the beginning to force the local
inhabitants to participate in the political task of
revolution, under Red leadership. There is called the
usual meeting of workers, peasants, and soldiers, under
the direction of the political officers accompanying
the Red Army organization, for the purpose of establishing
a soviet. The "enemies of the people" are brought before
a popular court for sentence;[64] all documents are
destroyed in a clean sweep, together with the landmarks
on the fields to be confiscated, and there is effected
a re-distribution of land among the poorer peasants and
workers; stores of rice and grain are immediately
confiscated by the new Government, and the price of food
commodities drastically lowered; the exchange rate between
copper and silver currencies is arbitrarily altered to the
benefit of the former (and, thus, of the poor who are its
chief users); finally, there is the promulgation of land
and labor laws, and the organization of trade-unions and
worker-peasant associations and organs. It is necessary

---

64. It is related that the same procedure prevailed in
the case of the death of General Chang Hui-tsan at
Tungku. ".... the Government troops knew that their
general was carrying silver and notes sufficient to
pay them. He had been carrying it for months .....
The troops entered Tungku because the communists
evacuated it. The Communists, fully aware of the
mutinous condition of the regulars, attacked. The
regulars laid down their arms without a fight ....
Between the rank and file of the regulars and the
Communists there was a spirit of 'hailfellow, well
met.' The Communists .... paraded the troops and
asked them what they wanted done with their general.
They pointed out they did not want to kill unneces-
sarily. Good men they were prepared to leave alive.
Was this general a good man? They asked those in
favor of his death to hold up their hands. The whole
division held up both hands. The general was, therefore, hacked to pieces before their eyes." (NORTH
CHINA DAILY NEWS, February 9, 1931.)

to recognize that such an introduction of Communist
doctrine to the poor peasant group that comprises
some 70% of the agrarian population would result in
considerable popular support being given to the
political organization effecting such a program.
This is particularly true when the Kuomintang offers
only execrations of the Reds to meet the challenge of
their revolutionary philosophy.

The two lines along which the Soviet groups have
been able to take effective action are in connection
with land distribution and taxation. Important
difficulties have been encountered in connection with
instituting changes in the ownership in land, just as
in the case of the U. S. S. R., the main questions
being what land should be confiscated, and whether
re-distribution should be on bare numerical basis or
whether ability to work the land should be a deciding
factor. A set of "Questions and Answers" for use in
Red discussion groups, got by a dike worker in the
Kienli section, states that the contemplated land
revolution

> "is the transference of all land from the posses-
> sion of the local tyrants, landowners, and userers,
> who constitute the propertied class, to the great
> agrarian masses, in order to get rid of all the
> special rights and exploitation in the villages,
> so that the peasant masses can obtain economic and
> political emancipation."

One of the chief difficulties arises, of course, in
classifying the peasants into "rich", "middle", and
"poor". The initial troubles by the experienced Soviets
in this respect, and in the later re-distribution, have
not yet been entirely eliminated, with the result that

the reorganization has often resulted in a lowering of
the total productivity because the fields have been
indiscriminately given to those unable to properly
cultivate them.[65]   Collectivisation was also attempted
in some cases by over-enthusiastic Communist leaders,
but a curb has been placed on this development.   No. 32A
of the Noulens documents, comprising a letter of instructio
under date of April 5, 1931, from the Pan-Pacific Trade-
union Secretariat to the All-China Labor Federation (ACLF),
referred to a section in the Draft Plan of the work for
trade-unions in the Soviet districts which read:

> '....We must determinedly (sic) oppose any attempt
> at the immediate introduction of the collective
> farms'.   It was suggested that there be added the
> condition: 'Unless such efforts at collectivisation
> are taken on the initiative of the peasants them-
> selves and is absolutely voluntary on the part of
> the peasants and without compulsion from the outside',

but there is little probability that large-scale collectivisation will be attempted in the near future.   The set
of "Questions and Answers" above-mentioned gives the
proper method of classification of the village peasants
as follows:

> "Besides the local tyrants, gentry, and the land-
> owners, there are the rich farmers, middle peasants,
> poor peasants, and hired laborers. This classifi-
> cation is made with regard to their relation to the
> land, their position in production, and actual
> conditions in each village."   A "rich farmer" is
> defined as one who belongs to the capitalist class
> in the village. "Anyone owning comparatively more
> and better land, who ordinarily exploits hired
> labor, or engages in trade, loans money at a high
> rate of interest, is grasping in money matters, and
> whose annual income exceeds his expenditures..."

A middle peasant, who, according to the current doctrine,
is considered a potential friend of the Soviets just as

---

65. See for a discussion of this the SOVIET TRI-DAILY,
    April 13, 1931; THE CHINA FORUM, January 27, 1932.

are the petit bourgeoisie,

> "is one whose annual income is just sufficient
> to meet the expenses of his family, who himself
> toils alone and does not exploit others; or
> one who has a large family of which few members
> can labor most being either old or young, who
> needs to employ a year-laborer but does not live
> extravagantly, or one who occasionally needs to
> employ a day-laborer whose (annual) total labor
> does not amount to that of a year-laborer." And,
> "A well-to-do middle peasant is one who relies
> on his own labor, and whose income, when the
> year is a good one, exceeds slightly his annual
> expenses and whose living is slightly liberal."

The land of the middle peasant is ordinarily considered to be his share in his character of "an ally of the laborers and poor peasants", but, depending upon local conditions, small amounts of his land may upon occasion be taken from him, or in the distribution he may be given some of the worse land. Red soldiers and their families, on the other hand, are given preferential treatment in the distribution of the land; moreover, it is proposed that "In addition, a common farm for the Red Army as a whole should be set apart, and laborers and peasants should be mobilized to till it for them, to meet the needs of the Red troops." After the confiscation of the rich farmer's land, stock, farm equipment, cash reserves, and foodstuffs, for the benefit of the community, he is to be given "a small piece of very poor land", unless he has been concerned in the anti-Red struggle and is classified as an "enemy of the people". It is stated that the amount of land one would have to own before being designated as a "rich farmer" cannot be definitely stipulated, depending as it does upon local conditions, including the density of population and fertility of the soil.

The Soviets take no half-way measures in the matter
of the taxes in force at the time of the arrival of the
Red government. All the existing imposts are abolished,
with the substitution instead of a graduated single tax
which falls the heaviest on the upper social strata.
Poor and middle peasants under the Western Fukien Soviet
regime are said to pay a land tax equal to 5% of the
harvest while rich farmers pay 15-30%. Traders presumably
pay proportionately. There are "Worker-Peasant Banks"
under the Kiangsi, Fukien, and Honan Soviet Governments,
issuing their own script as well as performing other
necessary functions of finance.

These measures concerning land and taxes, are designed
above all others to get the support of the land-hungry
tenant-peasant, oppressed as he is by the parasitism of
an omnivorous militarism. Before the Reds ever come in
with their full organization, there have usually been
attempts to rally the peasants into a fight against the
payment of ground rents and debts, the organization
sometimes taking the form of secret Red peasant groups.
In southern China, the percentage of tenant farming
averages 60%, and in some places is as high as 80%; the
usual rent is on a share basis - 50%-50%, with there
being sometimes stated a specific minimum amount that
must be paid, good crop or no; and interest rates run up
as high as 100% per annum, so that the term "usury",
commonly found in Communist propaganda, is often more
than a mere figure of speech. A striking picture of the
composition of the agrarian population of China was given
by Mo Cheh-tung, a peasant leader of the 1924-6 period:

"The small landlord class number something
over two million persons i.. led and organized
principally by the big landlords, and by the
village gentry and 'elders'. The main body of
the peasantry number about 320 million. Of
these the most conservative are the yeomanry
(working farmers owning their own farms), about
120 million strong. Of this group, not more
than 10 per cent. (sic) or 12 million, have any
economic surplus... About half, or 60 million,
are just holding their own and making a living;
these are usually timid, trying to avoid
struggles. The remaining 48 million of the
yeomanry are farmers who are losing ground each
year and rapidly going into bankruptcy. These
latter, althouth unreliable, definitely tend to
support the revolutionary struggle. The main
force of the revolutionary peasantry consists
of the semi-yeomanry, the tenants, together with
the village poor. These total more than 170
million... Then there are the "lumpen proletarians"
of the villages. These are the people who have
been squeezed entirely off the land, who are unable
to migrate to the cities, and who starve and rot
in idleness and crime. They furnish the nucleus
and reserve for recruitment of soldiers, bandits,
thieves, beggars and prostitutes... They number
about 20 million."[66]

The Soviet Government has concerned itself with more
than land and financial problems, however. The soviet
at Chingkangshan was destroyed by Government troops in
1929, whereupon the Chu Teh and Mao Tse-tung combination
moved its Peasant-Labor Committee and Kiangsi Soviet
Government organs to Tungku; "Lenin schools, People's
Equality Bank, and all that there ought to be there was,
going to make up the basic region for Kiangsi."[67] A
comment on the conditions existing in Kiangsi in 1931 is
found in Peck's report from Nanking on November 24, 1931:

"An American citizen who has recently traveled in
Hupeh, Kiangsi, and other Yangtze Valley provinces,
informed an officer of the Consulate General on
November 24, 1931, that from information gathered
from American missionaries and other persons, he
believed that there was a Communist state with a
solid block of territory in southern Kiangsi, that
it had adequate revenues (it was reported to have
Chinese $12,000,000 in cash reserves), and that the
peasants were contented under its sway. The property
of the wealthy, he said, had been distributed among
former tenantry, and terrorist methods had been to a
great extent abandoned."

66. Fang Fu-an, Chinese Labor, p. 18-19.
67. TA KUNG PAO, January 7, 1931.

Besides the action taken concerning land and finance, certain other Soviet measures may be listed as follows:

a: Education. In all established Soviet districts, there are the Lenin schools, in which were disseminated doctrines of Marxism and Leninism to the population. In the Juichin area, there are also middle schools and schools for adult education. Fukien, Kiangsi, and the Hung Hu district, at least, have schools for the education of prospective Red Army leaders, as well as training schools for the development of political propagandists and organizers. There are published regular newspapers, as well as the wall-newspaper that is so much used in the U. S. S. R. for purposes of popular education. Propaganda work among the regular troops is very active; it is charged by the Communists that White troops entering Red territory commonly have a squad of illiterate soldiers clean up all placards and handbills before the arrival of the main body of troops.

b: Social Mores. The Soviets work to place men and women on a plane of absolute equality. The sexes are both enfranchised, and hold equally the right to office in the Soviet organization. They also have equal obligations in the matter of communal production and military defense, serving in the Red Army if necessary.[68]

---

68. Note the case of Ho Lung's sisters participating in the military campaigns in Hupeh. There is also said to be a woman cavalry leader under Ho Ying, as well as various women among her troops. It seems improbable, however, that the Reds have any cavalry, although they have two or three airplanes that they cannot use.

Likewise, they are paid equally for equal work.   There
is the advocacy of freedom in marriage, with the abolition
of the custom of "gift-money" which requires the groom-to-
be to present a large sum of money to the mother of his
fiancee; liberal divorce policies are followed.

The land and property of monasteries is generally
confiscated, the buildings being converted into offices
for the soviets. The policy toward religion is based on
the Communist assumption that "Religion is the opiate of
the people", so that the anti-religious phase is an
essential part of the revolutionary movement.

c: Labor Legislation. Inasmuch as the Soviets thus
far have been chiefly concerned only with small manufacturing
and cottage industry, and agricultural labor, there has
been very little scope for the application of labor
legislation. Nevertheless, there are always promulgated
certain fundamental rules, to indicate the goal. The
working-day shall not exceed 8 hours, and the worker is
entitled to a minimum wage for his labor. These are the
fundamental desiderata, it being incumbent upon State
enterprises to adhere to them. For the achievement of the
goal in private enterprise, the development of labor unions
is pushed, with every effort made to force the gradual
accordance of the entrepreneurs with these essentials.
There are besides, legal provisions looking toward the
protection of labor in its relations with capital.

----

69. In the agreement between the Kienli Soviet Government
    and the administrators of dike reconstruction in Hupeh,
    it was stipulated by the Communists Committee on Dike
    Reconstruction that "Male and female laborers shall
    receive equal wages. When a child laborer does similar
    work he must receive similar wages."

d: Communal Institutions: There is the provision
of the communal working of the land held for the
benefit of the Red soldiers, and it is stated that, at
least in Fukien, it is decreed that the forests and
mines are the property of the whole people, to be worked
by the State. There is evidently the policy of developing
the cooperative movement, in the matter of both factories
and shops, but there is no attempt to do away with private
enterprise as such, or even to restrict the bourgeois
entrepreneur more than by depriving him of his rights
of franchise, so long as he accords to Soviet laws. Again
the pattern would seem to be one that makes use of the
Russian experience. There are ordinarily, however,
public rice-granaries and the fixing of the price of
grain, and the control of other prices. There seems to
be little doubt that the price of rice, in particular, is
usually lower in Soviet districts than elsewhere, and
that other supplies are fairly reasonable.[70]

There is an attempt at communal hospitalization, but
the Reds are badly handicapped by the lack of medicines
and doctors.[71]

---

70. For instance, Rev. Skinsnes writes on March 26, 1932,
from Hsinyang to the effect that the Communists sell
rice from their stores at Chiliping, at the rate of
380 cash for 3 "chin", and meat at 20¢ per "chin";
for rice, this is one-fourth the Hankow market price,
and for meat, one-half. In Honan there is an issue
of grain once a month. Rev. Skinsnes also states
that other things sold are reasonable in price.
71. Father Turk, captured by the Reds in Hupeh in 1931,
when released by them requested permission of his
superior to return to the Soviet area in the Hung Hu
region with facilities for establishing a hospital
among them, because of the dire need of the people
and the many wounded Red soldiers for medical care.
Permission was refused. There is at least one hospital
run by the Soviets in that area, but its facilities are
far from adequate.

e: People's Organizations. The implicit purpose of the Soviets is to organize all the people of the community so that each participates in the economic production and consumption, and in the political administration. Theoretically, no economic or social measures must be taken without the sanction of popular approval. There are, in the first place, the village and district "public centers", where all gatherings are held. Starting at the very lowest rung on the ladder, there are organized Poor Peasants' groups, then on an ascending scale such organizations as the Agricultural Workers' Unions, and labor-unions, affiliated with the ACLF. There are women's organizations, Red Pioneer groups (children less than 15 years of age), the Young Communist League (YCL), and the Communist Party itself; members of other revolutionary groups, such as the Anti-Imperialist League, et cetera, may or may not be found in the several soviets.

f: Red Military Organization. Where early in the struggle there was very little cooperation between the several Red guerilla groups, the growth of the military strength of the Soviets has resulted in the closer knitting together of the organization until there is now communication, and considerable cooperation, between the several armies. Communication is partly by messenger, but the important groups also have military radio sets, described by them as "gift presented by the enemy". The Red Armies are under the control of the CCP. Ho Lung and Chu Teh, with the assistance of Mao Tse-tung, would seem to be in control of the general military strategy of the Red armies, but for the present there are in reality two large battle regions, as divided by the Yangtze River. Chu Teh is first in control in the south, and Ho Lung in the north, but it is assumed that there would be coordination of the two forces in the event of a "big push" for a victory in the middle Yangtze region.

The largest unit is the Army (軍), or Corps, until recently ordinarily comprising no more than 5,000 men except in the case of certain important leaders. Considerable confusion in the numerical designations given by the press to the several Red units, and other evidence would indicate, however, that there has recently been a reorganization and a consolidation into larger armies (seven?), for the fighting of more important battles than could be done formerly when it was necessary to gather together a large number of comparatively small units of partisans. This need for heavier troops wouldbe a function of the growing importance of the Soviet regions. If this is true, the former "armies" would have become divisions in some cases, to be parts of a consolidated Red Army of perhaps 20,000 men under some important leader.

The military organization within the Army follows the usual divisions, excepting that there are no brigades, the next category after the division being the regiment. The number of regiments in a division varies, but there are 3 battalions in a regiment and 3 companies in a

battalion. There is often added a company of Vanguards
or Red Guard shock troops. Men and officers are on an
equal basis as far as food and pay is concerned, but
there is rigid discipline.[72] As regards pay, there is
a conflict of testimony which would seem to indicate
that the rate of remuneration depends upon the comparative
prosperity of the organization. The rate usually stated
is $20 per month, "from horse-coolie to general", but
the tendency is evidently toward a general rule whereby
most of the avilable Soviet money is used for the purchase
of essential supplies, the individual soldiers and officers
being given only a food allowance, which may be no more
than 10 cents per day.[73]   "Squeeze" of funds is punished
by shooting.[74]

To every military organization there is attached a
Political Officer and a political organ, for political
organization, propaganda, and direction. There are said
to be also "schools", for military and political training
in each Army. The political and military officers are
theoretically equal in authority.

Besides the regular Red troops, there are the Red
Guards, who are in effect the Red militia. The Army
and the Guards are supported in battle by the peasant
organizations and by the Youth Vanguard of the YCL, and
other volunteer groups. The first wave of storm troops
is ordinarily composed of the volunteer and peasant

72. Besides his military discipline, the Red soldier in
    Kiangsi has 8 obligations in his relations with the
    populace; to 'close the door, to tie the straw, to
    return all things that are borrowed, to repay all the
    things that are damaged, to do business fairly, to
    talk peacefully, to perform natural functions at
    proper places and not to pilfer the pocket of a "white"
    soldier.' CHINA FORUM, January 27, 1932.
73. ibid.
74. TA KUNG PAO, February 11, 1932.

groups, the main weight of the Guard and Army strength being the second wave of the attack.

g: Soviet Government. The Soviet Government is organized on the basis of province (省), hsien (縣), district (區), locality (鄉), and village (村). The governmental agencies of the locality and village are established directly by mass meeting, while the province, district, and hsien governments are established through the action of a meeting of delegates. The system of election is patterned after the Russian Soviet system, under the Chinese system there being first a delegate for every five workers and peasants (one delegate for 40 Red soldiers), with the process of consolidation up through the localities resulting in a representation in the hsien of one delegate for 1000 people (one delegate for every 300 Red soldiers). In the Hupeh area, there is said to be a general conference of delegates twice yearly, there is no provision for the regular convocation but of all-China congresses. The administrative duties fall within the realm of the Executive Committee of the Soviet Government, which comes into existence by the will of the popular congress. It is headed by a Chairman, and has under it various committees effecting the administratic of government, in the realm of military affairs, and supplies, education and propaganda, finance, industry, social affairs, agrarian problems, et cetera, each Committe being headed by a Commissioner (主 任). It is stated that up to this time there have been formed 500 soviets in southern and central China.[75]

75. Tokyo Report, op. cit., p. 16.

As regards the personnel of the Chinese Soviet
system, it is essential to recognize that the leaders
of the Red Armies, and the leaders in the Soviet
organizations, are educated men, confirmed in their
revolutionary beliefs. In a conversation with Peck
on July 20, 1931, Yang Hsing-fo (Yang Chien), Secretary-
General of the Academia Sinica, informed the Councillor
that the Red forces in Kiangsi have thousands of
trained military officers; some of them are Whampoa
graduates who could not be given positions in the
National Army, and others are men who had been sent to
the U. S. S. R. by the Canton Government for purposes
of study and on their return found that the Nationalist
Government was no longer sympathetic with Communism.[76]
The great dearth of employment for the intelligentsia
in the present-day social system of China, in combination
with the appalling economic and political state of the
country, tends to throw a large number of the educated
Chinese into the ranks of revolution. Rev. Bly, of
the United Lutheran Mission at Huangchuan, Honan, states
that probably all of the important leaders in the Honan-
Anhui-Hupeh Soviet organization are graduates of
universities and colleges, at least one being a returned
student from France; some of these were associated with
the Hankow Government in 1926-7, and had to flee for
their lives at the time of the turn-over. Rev. Kristofer
Tvedt, captured October 17, 1930, at Loshan, Honan, after
his release gave similar testimony:

---

76. Peck, July 23, 1931.

> "The so-called bandits which held them are
> actually well-disciplined Communists, Rev.
> Tvedt said. He said that many Chinese youths,
> educated in the United States, England, Germany
> and other places are among their leaders."[77]

Rev. Andersen, captured in 1931 at Kingmen by Ho Lung,

gave similar information concerning the organization

of his captors. His statements were corroborated by

the account of Miss Nelson, who with another woman

missionary was captured at the same time and released

on the advice of Ho Lung's foreign educated advisers:

> "They travelled for days before they reached
> General Ho Lung's headquarters. He was very
> friendly, and assured the ladies no harm would
> come to them. He explained earnestly that he
> was not a 'bandit' but the leader of an organized
> Communist army. Discipline was well preserved,
> and those who violated regulations, including
> opium-smoking, were summarily shot. At General
> Ho's headquarters, the ladies found several
> Chinese secretaries educated abroad or in mission
> schools. One political adviser is a graduate of
> Yale-in-China. Two physicians, once connected
> with mission hospitals in Honan and Hunan, seem
> to have much influence in the camp."[78]

Father Kreutzen, who spent the month of November 1930

in captivity by the Reds in eastern Hupeh, reported on

his return that he had not been badly treated by his

captors:

> "He states that the Communists in south-east
> Hupeh comprise a very strong organization with
> connections all along the river and with
> headquarters in Hankow. A number of their
> leaders were educated abroad and have been
> thoroughly inoculated with Soviet doctrines,
> and are inoculating the country folk."[79]

Intelligent Chinese, denied the possibility of economic

and political betterment for the country through the

medium of an honest and democratic form of government,

---

77. UNITED PRESS, April 22, 1931.
78. United PRESS, May 1, 1931.
79. REUTER, December 6, 1930.

have turned in hard desperation to revolution for a
solution of their problems. In China today the
movement of the discontented masses is led by those
who would probably have been willing to participate
in a liberal Left Government, but who now accept
Communist principles as those offering the greatest
possibilities for the elimination of corruption in
government, and for the rehabilitation of a social
system in which the people now exist in grinding
poverty. A bare recital of the structure of a
revolutionary organization is apt to give a distorted
impression of its comparative importance in the
national picture, but significance of the activities
of the Soviets in China should not be underestimated.[80]

IV. THE CHINESE COMMUNIST PARTY

1. Organization.

The organization of the CCP, being entirely underground, is very naturally difficult to trace. Holcombe
states that at the time of the 1925 (CCP) convention
the CCP had less than 1,000 members.[81] In 1924, before
admission into the Kuomintang, the CCP numbered only 40
members. At the convention in May 1927, when the
leadership was in the hands of Ch'en Tu-hsiu (   ),

---

80. For general information concerning the actions of the
    Soviets in China, see especially: Tokyo Report, op.
    cit.; Yang Chien, op. cit.; Mif, op. cit.; THE CHINA
    FORUM, January 27, 1932; INTERNATIONAL PRESS CORRES-
    PONDENCE, December 18, 1930; TA KUNG PAO, April 4,
    1931, February 11, 1932. For an account of the rise
    of Chu Teh and Mao Tse-tung to power, from the capture
    of Nanchang until the middle of 1931, see TA KUNG PAO,
    July 14, 1931. For a Russian view of the present
    significance of Soviets, See E. Iolk "New Victory
    of the Chinese Soviets"; PRAVDA, November 4, 1931.
81. THE CHINESE REVOLUTION, p. 209.

who cooperated with the Indian Communist Roy and with Borodin, there was reported an official membership of over 50,000. There was a heavy decline in membership immediately following the split with the Kuomintang in 1927, so that the membership dropped as low as 17,000 by the beginning of 1930.[82] With the successive civil wars and consequent disillusionment of the student group in the country, however, and with the successes of the Red armies against the Kuomintang troops, the cause of revolution in China has grown stronger despite the many attacks upon it. The Communist movement has strong adherents in the several universities and colleges of the country, particularly in Shanghai, Peiping, Canton, and Tientsin. There seems to be reliable evidence of the existence in the Wuhan area of a skeleton Communist organization, despite the frequent "cleansings" to which the cities have been subjected. No Communism is reported from the country distric in Szechuan, but the students in the Chengtu schools are reported to be infected with Red doctrines. In the transport and communication services throughout the country, and in the mines, the CCP has also gained in strength. It is probable that the present strength is over 100,000,[83] exclusive of the YCL membership, with most of the numerical strength concentrated in the Soviet districts. But, the CCP organs directing the activities of the Party are located in Shanghai.

---

82. Tokyo Report, op. cit., p. 5.
83. cf. Snow, "The Bolshevist Influence", CURRENT HISTORY, January 1931, p. 521.

In the latter part of January 1931, 40 Communists
were arrested by the Settlement police in Shanghai,
and it was reported that there had been discovered a
plot for an uprising on February 6th. Considerable
evidence was captured in the raids. In May (?), the
police in Singapore arrested Joseph Ducroux (alias
Serge Lefrance), a French Communist, getting in the
raid a list of names and other information concerning
revolutionary activities in the Far East. With the
assistance of the material thus acquired, the Shanghai
police were enabled to arrest the Rueggs Couple (alias
Noulens, et alia) on June 15th, seizing still more
documents relating to Communist activity in China,
Japan, the Philippines, the Straits Settlements, and
the Dutch East Indies, indicating that Shanghai was
probably a headquarters for the revolutionary movement
in the Far East. As the result of this arrest, on June
22, 1931, there were caught Hsiang Chung-fa (向 忠 發),
Chairman of the Central Committee (CC) and known as the
"Stalin of China", Chou En-lai (   ) - another
CC member - and several others.[84]   Hsiang Chung-fa and
Chou En-lai were executed the following day, on the
direct orders of Chiang Kai-shih; Ducroux in Singapore

---

84. The police also apparently received some assistance
    in making the June arrests from the revelations made
    by Kuo Chen-ch'ang (   ), a former member of the
    CC of the CCP, who was arrested in Hankow in April 1931.
    He renounced his Communist connections and gave the
    police important information concerning the activities
    and organization of the Party, in return for which
    apostasy he was spared his life and given a position
    with the Nanking Government. The bodies of seven
    murdered members of Kuo's family were discovered buried
    in a garden in the Shanghai French Concession in
    November 1931; the bodies of four others of his rela-
    tives were found by the police later.

was sentenced to 18 months in prison for Communistic activities; Paul and Gertrude Rueggs were extradited to the Chinese military authorities and are still in prison awaiting trial. About the middle of August, Teng Yen-ta (鄧演達),former head of the Political Training Department of the Hankow Government and generally known as the right-hand man of Borodin, was taken into custody in the French Concession in Shanghai. Lu Hsiung-yi (   ), said to be a member of the CC of the CCP, and 12 others were captured at the same time. These revolutionaries were also extradited to the Chinese military, and subsequently executed.

This series of arrests was a severe blow at the leadership of the CCP, and doubtless resulted in a radical tightening-up of the Communist secret organization. According to the Tokyo Report, the present actual power resides in the hands of Li En-mei (   ), Ch'en Tse-min (   ), Cheng Hung-yi (   ), Hsiang Ying (項 英), and several others.

The orders of the CCP organization in Shanghai go directly to the Red military and Soviet organs in the field. Ho Lung is a Red military leader whose name appears frequently in the Noulens documents as one with whom there is frequent communication, and he is named in the same papers as President (Chairman?) of the Central Revolutionary Committee. Rev. Andersen, a former captive of the Red Leader, states that Ho Lung informed him that the Red Army received orders direct from Shanghai; there is, moreover, evidence of a Communist organization in Hankow for the purpose of coordinating Red activities

in the area, and for the purchase of supplies.   Chu
Teh and Mao Tse-tung of Kiangsi are referred to in the
Noulens documents as Acting Presidents (Chairmen?) of
the Central Revolutionary Committee.   This trio would
seem to be the chief termini of the CCP ramifications
centering in Shanghai.

The Noulens documents also give information to the
effect that the members of the Central Bureau in April
1931 were Chu Teh, Tseng Ping-ch'un (曾 炳 春), Ch'en
I (陳 毅), Chou I-li (   ), P'eng Teh-huai,
and Lin Piao (林 彪).

There are now, and have been since 1927, important
schisms in the ranks of the Communists themselves, the
conflict sometimes being characterized as primarily a
counterpart of the Stalin-Trotsky feud.   The original
quarrel may have been along the lines of the Russian
split, but there are indications that, due to the fact
that the problems of China are primarily its own and
the differences between the Stalin and Trotsky ideologies
are of little significance in the Oriental background,
the quarrel in the CCP lies along other lines.   The
Opposition in the CCP seems to comprise a group that might
be characterized as Second Internationalists.   As indicated
above, there are many persons in the Communist movement in
China who would probably have fallen into the ranks of the
Left-wing parliamentarians, had happier conditions prevailed

---

85. Ho Lung himself is reported to have made a visit in town
in the Spring of 1932, and a Catholic Father was recently rather disagreeably surprised to come face to face
with a Red officer, his sometime captor, in the dining-
room of the leading Hankow hotel.   Another Catholic Father
states that two Red officers recently made a trip to a
town to buy certain supplies from the garrison troops.

in the country. Many of the present-day Reds are elements

that were with the Hankow Government when it reached a

disastrous end after a promising arrival in the Yangtze

valley.[86] Not all those in the Communist movement are

entirely in sympathy with some of its more radical policie

Ch'en Tu-hsiu, the leader of the CCP during the peri

---

86. With reference to the character of the Canton group,
which prior to its accession to power in Hankow was
stigmatized by the foreign and native press of the
country as "Red" and "Bolshevist", it is interesting
to note that Lockhart reported from Hankow that:
"There is no evidence at hand thus far that the
Revolutionary Army is particularly unfriendly towards
Americans... My contacts with officials of the new
regime, while they have been few so far, have been
agreeable. The officers appear to be bright and
intelligent men who are inspired with much zeal and
a well-defined idea as to what it is that they are
trying to accomplish. An atmosphere of security is
being cultivated, and the Chinese as well as foreigne
are becoming more reconciled to the turn of affairs a
are beginning to feel that perhaps the Cantonese are
more capable of establishing and maintaining in this
area a responsible Government than any other regime
that has recently attempted it." (Monthly Political
Report, September 20, 1926). Lockhart's impressions
of a year later were reported by Mayer from the
Legation: '. The economic and financial fabric of
the Yangtze Valley is little short of being in a
state of complete ruin. 2. The Chinese people have
lost confidence in their leaders and in a large
measure in some of the principles with which they wer
inspired to a patriotic endeavor to rescue the countr
from its present condition of disorganization and
irresponsibility... 7. Financial affairs are so con-
fused that it is hopeless soon to expect any order
out of the present chaos. 8. The military has arisen
to its old order of supreme authority with its auto-
cratic and cruel exactions from the people.' (Legatio
Monthly Political Report, October 27, 1927) Without
denying the excesses of boisterous leaders in their
new-found revolutionary strength, it is necessary to
note that the break between the Chiang Kai-shih group
and the Nationalist Government came in March 1927, an
the Government in its Hankow form came to an end in
July of that year.

of its cooperation with the Kuomintang, became the Trotsky
of the CCP upon his expulsion from the Party in 1927 because
of his "opportunism" - one of the chiefest of Communist
crimes after "deviation"! Ch'en Tu-hsiu probably has at
this time a small following, but it would not be one
constituting much of an Opposition group. Ch'en himself
was an "intellectual" Communist of the theoretical type,
a former associate of Hu Shih, whereas the strategic
requirements of the moment demand strong action along some
definite line, from any political group that would survive.
There is evidence that the students are beginning to
discover that theorizing is not enough, and are desirous
of giving expression to their energies in other form.
The successor to Ch'en Tu-hsiu was Li Li-san, who himself
lost power because of his "adventurism" and was followed
(probably) by Hsiang Chung-fa. But Li Li-san is still in
the CCP.

The dissenting particles in the Party apparently take
overt form at present in the "AB Union", which evidently
has given considerable trouble to the orthodox Communists.
If one were to believe the Government reports, the "AB
Union" has on several occasions brought the Communist
organization to the point of dissolution, with of course
considerable bloodshed. This is evidently not entirely
true, but this Union was reliably reported to have been
responsible for some trouble among the Reds at Futien
(Kiangsi), in particular, and various reports have come out
of southern Honan to the effect that the same clique is not
without power in the Soviet organization there. Its exact
nature and orientation are not at all clear, but it is
thought that the "AB Union" may be the outward expression of
the tendency, outlined above, of a deviation of some of

the Leftist elements toward a more moderate policy.

Nor, apparently, can all the Red military leaders be trusted to follow faithfully the tenets of Communism. Huang Kung-lueh and P'eng Teh-huai have at various times had aspersions cast upon their loyalty. Ho Lung, too, has been said to be a doubtful element in the Red organization, as, for that matter, have many others. Fu Po-ts'ui (傅柏翠), who for four years held power in south-western Fukien in the name of the Reds, announced his allegiance to Nanking in June 1931.[87] However, any revolutionary movement in its inception is much more liable to division into "jarring sects", than it is after it has later got started along the road to power, when it is obvious that union is necessary for success against the enemy. There may be serious schism after partial success has been achieved (as was the case after the Kuomintang left Canton for the march on Peking), but it is probable that, if the successes of the Reds continue to mount and influence to spread, the adherence of the various elements to the Red revolutionary movement will become stronger in the face of the sufferings of the people and the moral collapse of the Kuomintang. It is also well to remember that, besides the constant addition of graduates of Chinese and foreign universities

---

87. Berger reports from Swatow that Fu was not considered to be much of a Red by Chu Teh and Mao Tse-tung, because of his known unreliability, so that (Berger states) he would probably make a poor ally for Nanking. (Monthly Political Report, July 2, 1931). However, the Noulens documents evidence that the Communist leaders found themselves in considerable difficulties in the Fukien area as the result of the turn-over.

to the body of revolutionary leaders, there are specially-
trained workers being turned out for the task of revolution
in China, both by the Chinese Workers Communist University
and the Stalin Eastern Workers University in Moscow, and
by special training-schools in China itself.

There has never been any report, so far as is known,
of Russians being connected with any of the Honan-Hupei-
Anhui-Hunan Red groups. However, when the French colonial
troops assisted the Kuangsi army to re-capture Lungchow from
the (17?) Red Army in March 1930, the news report stated
that five (four?) Red Russians had been captured at that
time and executed. It is also stated that several Russians
were attached in an advisory capacity to the Haifeng (Kuangtung) Soviet Government in 1930, several of them being killed
in a skirmish with regulars on March 18th of that year; it
is also reported that several Russian Communists were
employed at the Red arsenal at Tungku.[88]   Russian names,
reforring to active agents in China, are found in the Noulens
documents. There is no doubt but that certain foreign Communists are actively working in the Chinese revolutionary
movement. Some of these Communists may very possibly be
connected with the Kiangsi organization, which is easy of
access through Fukien and which would attract those Occidentals
who wished to actively support the Chinese Soviet movement.
It is probable also that Comintern money for the support of
the Chinese revolutionary movement comes into the country
through Shanghai, the CCP being definitely affiliated with
that organization. However, Ducroux was French, and the
Rueggs are evidently some nationality other than Russian;
the Comintern itself is an international organization with

---

88. Tokyo Report, op. cit.

its headquarters in Moscow, and there seems to be no
reason for believing that any aid of money or men that
may arrive in China for the support of the revolutionary
movement has been sent by the Government of the U.S.S.R.
The revolution grows out of the fertile soil of China
itself - and would do so with or without aid from the
outside. The seed was a foreign import, but the product
is Chinese.

Thus far, the main strength of the Communist movement
has been in the peasantry and the student groups. The
Red trade-unions as yet have little organizational strength
in Chinese industry largely because of the measures of
repression by Kuomintang authorities. This discovers
the weakness of the CCP organization to be in that
part of the proletariat that was, in the case of Russia
in 1905 and 1917, considered the leading group of the
revolution - the town working-class. Of 3,000,000
industrial workers in China, the CCP has connections with
no more than 3,000. The chief Red strength is among
transport workers (on railways and waterways), and the
miners. The industry most highly developed and most
heavily manned in China - the textile industry - has
evidently thus far been but little penetrated by Communist
influence, because the workers are chiefly women and
children, who are at best conservative in tendency and
not inclined toward dangerous activities (as demonstrated
in the German elections). The Communist explanation of
this weakness in industry is that under the control of
Li Li-san the trade-union work was badly neglected,
accounting in part for the poor showing. It is of course

recognized by the Red leaders that the successful
organization of the industrial workers in the cities
would mean a great strengthening of the revolutionary
movement.

> "The problems of the further spreading of the
> struggle into new territory, the establishment
> of regular and centralized worker-peasant Red
> Armies, the establishment of a Central Soviet
> Government and the solid territorial bases of
> the Soviet movement, require the strengthening
> of the proletarian nuclei in the Soviet movement,
> but this in turn requires the further unfolding
> of the proletarian struggle in the important
> industrial centers of China." 89

There is evidently an increase in Communist activity in
trade-union work, and national crises such as the Sino-
Japanese situation provide an excellent screen for
subversive movements. For instance, some 20,000 workmen
met in Shanghai on January 17, 1932, under the auspices
of local anti-Japanese societies, and passed resolutions
calling for the following: 1) the arming of the people;
2) the overthrow of imperialism; 3) the organization of
true volunteer corps; 4) the organization of Citizens'
Courts; and 5) the protection of the Soviets in China.[90]
Student movements, beginning with the consideration of
questions of foreign relations, (for example), readily
become involved in adverse criticism of the Kuomintang
and demands for its overthrow; the next step is a
searching for the means for such overthrow. With the
widespread dissatisfaction with the Kuomintang rule, in
combination with the efforts of the CCP in the industrial
centers, it is probable that the trade-union movement
will be considerably strengthened in the comparatively

---

89. E. Iolk, op. cit., PRAVDA, November 4, 1931.
90. RENGO, January 19, 1932.

near future. It may be that the students will offer
leadership to the movement, as they did in 1922 and
1925.

2. Policy.

The statements and actions of the CCP have been
consistently along one revolutionary line from 1927
until the present. The first concrete expression of
the policy of the Party came with the uprising of
December 11, 1927, at Canton, as noted in a Russian
account:

> ".....the new revolutionary Power was able to
> show itself the real Power of the workers. The
> Canton Soviet succeeded in issuing decrees; for
> the 8-hour working day for the confiscation of
> all the landlords' lands and the turning over
> of them gratis to the peasants, for the annulling
> of all cabalistic debt and rent agreements. The
> Canton Soviet issued a dictum for the confiscation
> of the houses of the big bourgeoisie and landowners
> and the transfer of the workers into these houses.
> The Extraordinary Commission for the Struggle with
> the Counter-Revolution with the aid of the workers
> - and especially the women - effected numerous
> arrests of known reactionaries. There were executed
> about 700 enemies of the people.
> "In the first hours of its existence the
> Soviet applied with fraternal appeals to the Union
> of Socialist Republics and to all the international
> proletariat, announcing its devotion to the work
> of the world struggle for socialism." 91

The same writer remarked that:

> "In the slogans of the Canton Commune for the first
> time in the whole country there was declared the
> hegemony of the proletariat, of the Soviets as the
> form of the revolutionary-democratic dictatorship
> of the proletariat and peasantry."

But the revolutionary organizations in the cities were
crushed by the measures of suppression that were begun in
April 1927 and which became more harsh with the momentary
success of the forces of revolution in seizing control

91. E. Iolk, "The Fourth Anniversary of the Canton
Commune", PRAVDA, December 13, 1931.

of such an important center as Canton. It is reported
that, in Canton itself, in the several days of violent
repression that followed upon the uprising, 6,000
persons were killed with short shrift. In Hankow, the
executions were very heavy until the following April,
and all over the country every measure was taken to
eradicate all elements that might conceivably contribute
to the revolutionary movement in the cities among the
labor classes. It became evident to the leaders of the
CCP that the effort to seize power in the towns could
not be successful, due to the fact that the preparatory
work had thus far been insufficient. Beginning about
April 1, 1928, the Communist organization definitely
went underground, and efforts to lead the workers of
the country into an open struggle with the Government
were abandoned for the time being.

> "When the Sixth Congress of the Comintern was
> held in July, 1928, in Moscow, the Chinese Communist
> Party held its Sixth General Conference there under
> the guidance of the Comintern. At this Conference
> a thorough reorganization of the party was effected
> and a course of future action was determined upon,
> which was to concentrate all efforts upon converting
> the city workers and upon instilling radical doctrines
> among peasants and soldiers in order to achieve the
> revolutionary ends by the concerted action of both
> the urban and the rural forces." [92]

The headquarters of the CCP itself had been established
in Shanghai immediately after the break-up in July 1927.
When the Red Army began to achieve important successes in
1929 and after, the Party began to supply leadership and
direction to the scattered military groups. This work
became even more important after the beginning of the
civil war in 1930, when the direction of the Central
authorities and all the militarists was directed toward
the north and the pressure on the Red Army was released.

---

92. Tokyo Report, op. cit.

On February 15, 1930, the ACLF and the CC of the CCP
jointly issued a manifesto proposing that there should
be held a conference of delegates from all the Soviet
regions on May 30th. A conference was held May 20-24th
in the vicinity of Chenju near Shanghai, with fifty-four
delegates attending from the Soviet districts and
communist organizations throughout the country. Besides
land and labor laws and a program of military tactics,
a political platform was drawn up by the congress,
embodying ten points:

> "overthrow of imperialism and the socialization
> of all banks, factories, and railways; destruction
> of militarism in China; seizure of land from the
> landlords without compensation and the introduction
> of collective farming; abolition of all taxation
> except a single tax on land; freedom of press and
> speech and full right of assembly; the right of
> self-determination for the minor nationalities
> included within the Republic of China".[93]

The Conference also passed two resolutions - one providing
for the convening of a national conference of Soviet
delegates, and the other proposing the establishment of a
Central Soviet Government of China. One of the Noulens
documents states:

> "The First National Conference of Soviet Represen-
> tatives of Chinese labourers, peasants and soldiers
> is to be convened when the Chinese Soviet revolutiona
> movement under the leadership of the proletariat, is
> directed strongly against the reactionary administra-
> tion of the imperialistic Kuomintang and when the
> imperialistic Powers have allied with the Kuomintang
> militarists to attack the Soviet. The object of the
> conference is to unify and consolidate the Soviet
> political power throughout the country and to establi
> a supreme authority for laborers, peasants and soldie
> under the dictatorship of the Soviet Provisional
> Central Government."

The date for the All-China Conference of Soviet
Delegates was originally set for November 7, 1930, and

---

93. Maxwell Stewart, NATION, August 27, 1930;
    cf. Kuo, "On the First Congress of the Chinese Soviets"
    INTERNATIONAL PRESS CORRESPONDENCE, June 12, 1930.

on August 20th there was established the Central
Preparatory Commission to do the preliminary spade
work. At this time, however, because of the strong
repressive measures of the Government, the Acting
Permanent Secretariat found itself unable to function.
On September 10th, 30 persons met in the Plenary
Session of the Central Preparatory Commission and
decided to change the original date to December 11,
1930, in commemoration of the Canton revolt. There
was also discussed at this time the draft of the
fundamental law of the Soviet Republic, which would be
based upon "the independent authority of the worker-
peasant people, and the authority of the propertyless
class". Unexpectedly, apparently, the CCP on November
16th received orders from the Comintern which incorporated
decisions reached by that body on July 23, 1930. The
orders leveled strong criticism at the inflated outlook
of the CCP which led it to indulge in nation-wide
disturbances without due regard to practical tactics,
and at the slowness with which the primary work of
organization and instruction was proceeding; the orders
proposed that the CCP emerge from its lethargic state.
The Central Political Bureau (Politbureau) met on
November 25th, and completely accepted the recommendations
of the Comintern. Li Li-san, who until then had occupied
the directing position in the Party, was expelled from the
Central Politbureau, being replaced at that time by
either Hsiang Chung-fa or Chang Kou-shou (張 國 燾).
In a report of the reasons for the dismissal of Li Li-san,
Ch'ü Ch'iu-pai (   ), a member of the Politbureau,

stated that Li's fundamental mistake was in not recognizing
that military action should be the movement of the whole
people, he being chiefly concerned with the movement of
troops, so that there was only a great deal of empty
shouting and playing around the while the duty of arousing
the fighting ardor of the whole people was forgotten.[94]
Li Li-san was appointed Chairman of the Propaganda
Committee, and Chou En-lai Chairman of the Organization
Committee.[95]   The date of the Conference was next set for
February 1931, but, while the preparatory conference was
proceeding, the police descended upon the assembled
delegates in a hotel in Shanghai and arrested them all.
They were summarily shot, and the CCP was forced to begin
anew the work of preparation for the conference. At the
time the Chinese Communist Party issued a manifesto
addressed to the Kuomintang:

> "Our tasks and aim, which burn the hearts of
> millions, are higher than the hideous and dirty
> work of the imperialists. The execution of our
> workers will not stop us, the Conference will be
> held. Our future victory - this is your death.
> Remember this."[96]

The Conference was finally held on November 7, 1931,
at Juichin, Kiangsi, and a central government was establish
for the "Chinese Soviet Socialist Republic", under the tit
of "The Provisional Government of the Chinese Soviet Repub
This Government described itself as

> "A governing machinery entirely in the hands of
> the workers, peasants, soldiers, and all toilers
> of China, and replacing the imperialist-Kuomintang-
> landlord-bourgeoisie regime." Its platform is:
> "The immediate

94.   TA KUNG PAO, February 1(?), 1930.
95.   Tokyo Report op. cit., there seems to be some doubt,
      however, that Li Li-san received such an appointment
      in November 1930.
96.   Letter from Shanghai, "The First Conference of the
      Chinese Soviets", PRAVDA, December 23, 1931.

abrogation of all unequal treaties concluded
between the imperialist countries and the
landlord-bourgeoisie governments of China, the
repudiation of all foreign debts contracted by
the ruling class of China for the suppression
of the mass movement and massacre of the masses,
the unconditional rendition of all foreign
settlements, concessions and leased territories
now under control of the imperialists, the
immediate withdrawal of all imperialist land,
air and naval forces from Chinese soil, last
but most important of all, the confiscation of
all imperialist banks, factories, mines and
communication-transportation enterprises located
in China as the most effective measure to destroy
the imperialist domination, root and branch.
Furthermore, the Provisional Government of the
Soviet Republic of China declares that it will,
on no condition, remain content with the overthrow of imperialism in China but, on the
contrary, will aid as its ultimate objective in
waging a war against world imperialism until the
latter is all blown up." Treaties may be concluded
with imperialist countries "on the basis of complete
equality, and "nationals of such countries domiciled
in the Soviet territory may enjoy liberty and
freedom in carrying on trade, commerce and industry,
provided they do not run counter to the Soviet laws";
in the event of such violation, such acts "will
positively lead to forfeiture of all liberty accorded
to them and of all property in their possession."97

97. CENTRAL CHINA POST, November 25, 1931; see also
Letter from Shanghai, PRAVDA, December 23, 1931;
Mif, PRAVDA, November 12, 1931. A consideration
of the program outlined by Mif (who is one of
the foremost Russian authorities on the subject
of the Chinese revolution, with an opinion which
presumably carries considerable weight in the
councils of the Comintern) leads one to believe
that the Manifesto indulges in large part the
Communist weakness for sloganism; there is
apparently no intent in the minds of the Communist
leaders to embark immediately upon a disastrous
program of wholesale confiscation of the property
of either Chinese or foreign entrepreneurs, although
a strict control is outlined. So, the meat of the
Manifesto is probably in the last phrases: "nationals
of such (imperialist - EC) countries domiciled in
the Soviet territory may enjoy liberty and freedom
in carrying on trade, commerce and industry, provided
they do not run counter to the Soviet laws". The
experience of the U. S. S. R. would teach that the
more conciliatory policy would be the better, and
the Soviets in China are very evidently making much
use of the Russian experience, in general.

V. CONCLUSION

Only one thing will stop the growing wave of social revolution in China - the bettering of the economic conditions of the population. It is impossible to halt the flow of ideas that is impinging upon the consciousness of the people, and it is apparent that the solution of the problems of China will be a catastrophic one. Despite the many glib formulae that issue for "the economic development of the country", large numbers of the people of central China are starving to death. The floods of 1931, entailing a loss of 2 billion dollars and affecting a peasant population equal in numbers to the whole farm population of the United States, struck a blow at the impoverished people from which they could not recover alone

In its survey of the damage wrought by the flood, the Department of Agricultural Economics of the University of Nanking reached the conclusion that 1½ billion dollars were needed to meet the immediate minimum needs of the afflicted population for food and clothing, fodder for the farm animals, seed for planting spring crops, and repairs for buildings (45% of which were destroyed in the flood area).[98] At the same time, the financial resources of the Government had dwindled down to an amount insufficient to permit the carrying on of the normal processes of administration, and at the same time it was confronted by a war threat from both Kuangtung and Japan. It was unable to offer little more toward flood-relief than the grain it had bought on credit from the United States, and corruption in administration reduced the value of that.

98. PEKING AND TIENTSIN TIMES, January 20, 1932, for resume of the report.

The China International Famine Relief Commission
officers estimate that an average of at least 5,000
persons per hsien have died of starvation from November
up until the present in Hupeh. There are 69 hsien in
the province, giving a total of about 350,000 deaths
thus far. Famine has arrived on larger scale still in
northern Anhui, where Rev. Bostock, on relief work at
Pochow, states that the people are dying at the rate of
100 per day of starvation in <u>one</u> hsien where/he is working.[99]
Cannibalism has made its appearance in the area. In
Eastern Honan conditions are very bad. Rev. Lee writes:

> "The conditions among the poor have become increasing-
> ly worse. I have visited the country to the East
> and also to the South this spring and it is a pit-
> iable sight that one sees in many places. Bark from
> trees sells as food. Weeds that grow in streams and
> stagnant pools are pretty well cleaned out East of
> us. People have used it for food";

As concerns his station, Juning, "People have been dying
on the streets". The situation around the Tungting Lake
in northern Hunan is said by relief workers to be worse
than Honan, and it is probable that Kiangsu is comparable
to Anhui. A conservative estimate would put the deaths
from starvation in the Yangtze and Huai valleys at one
million up to date, and now the strength of the relief
work is spent. China International Famine Relief
Commission officers state that the planting has been
short, because of the scarcity of seed, so that the
famine will probably carry over into 1933. Many people
more will die in China before the effects of the flood
will have been repaired. And this is added to the famine

---

99. PEKING AND TIENTSIN TIMES, April 23, 1932.

conditions that already exist in Kansu, Chinghai, and Ninghsia.

Confronted with this situation, the Hupeh Bureau of Reconstruction by means of circulars has offered advice to the peasants; during the period of national emergency (the Sino-Japanese trouble) the peasants should:

> "(1) increase the production of foodstuffs: a) by the cultivation of unclaimed land, the utilization of waste land, the planting of more foodstuffs, and the prevention of disasters from floods, drought, and pests; b) by the cessation of poppy cultivation and the restriction of the production of non-edible crops such as tobacco; by the promotion of the cultivation in large quantities of such food articles as potatoes, et cetera.
> "(2) investigate foodstuffs – the kinds and quantity of foodstuffs produced locally, and storage and local consumption.
> "(3) store foodstuffs; local granaries should be re-established and new granaries begun.
> "(4) rear domestic animals in large numbers, paying special attention to such increased production.
> "(5) limit expenses. Brewing should be prohibited. Methods of provision-storage and grinding should be improved.
> "(6) start cooperative societies of all kinds in order to develop rural districts economically.
> "(7) use national commodities. Peasants should use national products so far as possible." 100

The emission of baseless programs will not fulfill the multifarious demands of the people, and the rate of development of the movement of protest, in the absence of economic progress, will be inversely to the amount of police pressure the Government can exert upon it. But, while ragged soldiers will fight an invader on hungry bellies, they will not effectively operate against the native population on the same terms. At the present time, the wages of the majority of the soldiery are in arrears fo

---

100. WUHAN JIH PAO, April 28, 1932.

period ranging from three to six months. The wages of
the 19th Route Army that fought so well at Shanghai
were about five months in arrears, and it is charged
that not even these arrears have been made up out of
the $3,000,000 sent to the Army by the people of the
country in recognition of their services. The troops
of Sun Lien-chung that revolted and joined the Reds were
unpaid for about four months. The two battalions of
Kao Kuei-tzu's troops that revolted at Pingting (Shansi)
in July 1931, killing their officers and raising the
red flag of the 24th Army, were unpaid soldiers. The
5th Division of the 2nd Army had revolted in Shansi
earlier in the year for the same reason, and mutinies
of troops are occurring in both Shansi and Honan at this
time. There have been large defections of troops at
various times during the last two years in Hupeh, where
at present the soldiers are getting $3.50 per month with
which to buy their food and shoes (a relief-laborer on
the dike reconstruction earns about $9.00 per month, in
terms of grain). It is probable that there will be
more and more troop revolts. The friendliness of the
troops to the Reds in the matter of supplying the latter
with munitions is well attested, and the Communist
propaganda carries a strong appeal to the unpaid soldier.
And, it is to be noted that, during the months of June
and July 1931, Communist organizers were sent north from
Shanghai to work among the troops as follows: Peiping 20;
Tangshan 5; Tientsin 5; Paoshu 10 and Pingtung 10
(among the troops of the 1st and 2nd Northeast Armies);
Shansi 30 (in the troops of Feng Yü-hsiang, Yen Hsi-shan,

Sun Tien-ying (孫殿英), and Kao Kuei-tzu (   );
northern Shensi 20 (for the troops of Ching Yueh-hsiu
(   ).[101] These facts indicate that the CCP is
making strong efforts to metamorphose the discontented
soldiers into Red troops.

The developments as regards impoverishment of the
population and the mutiny of the troops hinge upon the
question of the unity of the governmental structure of
the country. Thus far, the Sino-Japanese trouble in
Shanghai has caused a postponement of the inevitable
civil war, but, unless the Japanese again attack, the
imbroglio cannot be much longer delayed. That the
emasculated National Emergency Conference has done
nothing at all toward effecting a rapprochement between
the dissentious groups in China seems undeniable. In
the first place, the Conference limited discussion to
three items - Red suppression, flood-relief, and
resistance to Japan - in regards to which the Nanking
triumvirate had already settled upon respective policies.
The Communists were deprived of all civil rights, nothing
further can be done for the flood-sufferers, and the
Nanking Government will continue officially to rely upon
the League, and privately to anticipate that the United
States or the U. S. S. R. will be imbroiled in a war with
Japan, for the settlement of China's current dispute.
But the southern groups, comprising Li Tsung-jen, Pai
Ch'ung-hsi (白崇禧), Hu Han-min (胡漢民), Ch'en
Chi-t'ang, and Eugene Ch'en (陳友仁) have had none
of their indictments of the Nanking Government satisfied,
and stand in opposition to it as much as ever.

101. TA KUNG PAO, August 22, 1931.

On October 21, 1931, Feng Yü-hsiang sent a telegram
to the Canton group setting forth 13 points of policy
in the fields both of national affairs and foreign
relations, purposing for mutual agreement certain radical
changes in political structure and policy. The Nanking
Government accepted the least of them all: "(4) Removal
of the national capital to a suitable spot so as to
avoid the threat of the gunboats of the Imperialists."[102]
On August 31, 1931, it was decided at Chang Hsueh-liang's
conference in Peiping that Yen Hsi-shan and Feng were to
be persuaded to leave Shansi for a trip abroad; "Appropriate
measures will be adopted in the event of the warning being
ignored."[103] In the first part of October, Chang Hsueh-
liang wired to Chiang Kai-shih suggesting that Feng and
Yen be invited to come to Peiping for a conference for the
discussion of means of coping with the Manchurian situation;
Chiang acceded to the suggestion and appointed three
prominent delegates for the task of persuading Feng "to
come out to join the authorities in the work of national
salvation."[104] But no point of agreement could be found
between Feng and the Nanking-Loyang-Sian authorities, for
Feng called for a strong policy in both external and
internal affairs, and it was impossible even to find a way
of using him in the Shanghai affair. The resignation and
return of Chiang Kai-shih found Feng and Canton still in
opposition. Feng wished to fight the Japanese, but, finding
the politics connected with the Shanghai fighting not at all
to his liking, withdrew with a sore throat, whereupon Han
Fu-ch'ü (韓　復　榘) suggested that Feng be given the post

---

102. For Feng's 13 points, see PEKING & TIENTSIN TIMES,
        October 23, 1931.
103. ibid, September 5, 1931.
104. ibid, October 6, 1931.

of Pacification Commissioner at Loyang. Yang Hu-ch'eng
(楊虎城), Chiang's man in Shensi, immediately
resigned. The wire of appointment did not issue,
however, and Han Fu-ch'ü went into retirement with
stomach trouble, on the mountain opposite Feng's place
at Taishan. Yen Hsi-shan has been re-appointed Director-
General for Peace of Shansi and Suiyuan, but his delegates
as well as Feng's are in Canton "to keep in touch with
the situation". Yen has also sent gifts of money and
uniforms to Feng, and blankets and other Shansi products
to Shih Yu-san (石友三), who is now in Tsinan.

There is another interesting figure in the cordon
sanitaire that grows up around the Chiang-Soong-Wang
trio. In the latter part of November 1931, a circular
telegram was sent to the National Government urging that
Wu P'ei-fu (吳佩孚) be placed in command of military
action against foreign aggression, the signers including
important leaders of North-west China: Ma Lin (馬麟),
Acting Chairman of the Chinghai Provincial Government;
Chin Shu-jen (金樹仁), Chairman of the Sinkiang
Government; Ma Hung-pin (馬鴻賓), Chairman of the
Kansu Government; Liu Ts'un-hou (劉存厚), Defence
Commissioner for the Szechuan-Shensi Border; Teng Hsi-hou
(鄧錫侯), commanding the 28th Army; T'ien Sung-yao
(田頌堯), commanding the 9th Army; Lei Chung-t'ien
(雷中田), Peace Preservation Commissioner for Kansu;
Ma Wen-chü (馬文車), Acting Chairman of the Kansu
Government; and various divisional commanders.[105]

---

105. ibid., November 26, 1931.

But the Government did not want to fight, so did not
take advantage of the offer of advice. Wu P'ei-fu
proceeded north via Ninghsia and Suiyuan, finally
arriving at Peiping, where he is evidently working
for the accession to power. He, Feng, and Canton,
all desire a more positive policy, even though it costs
Chiang Kai-shih the three crack divisions that are now
his main reliance for his political influence. The
North and South are both against the Nanking Government,
though whether they will cooperate is as yet problematical.

Whether the Japanese fight or are inactive at
Shanghai, the direction of the Chinese State will
evidently be wrested from the hands of Chiang Kai-shih,
and that probably before the year is out. The whole,
then, is a triangular question, with revolution, civil
strife, and foreign relations the three points. Victory
for Japan is ultimately impossible, but the fighting may
proceed along several different lines. There is little
probability that the Communists would cooperate against
Japan in the first part of some hypothetical war in
China Proper, even though the leader were Feng Yü-hsiang,
but such a war would mean the growth of the revolutionary
movement (and possibly not in China alone), which would
finally be diverted into the anti-Japanese struggle. War
between the U.S.S.R. and Japan would probably stimulate
the forces of revolution in the country still more, for
there would not operate so strongly as in the case of a
Sino-Japanese war the forces of national feeling within
China to keep potential revolutionaries on the side of
the group fighting the foreigner. It may be pointed out

that the matter is not to be isolated within the boundarie
of the former Heavenly Kingdom. Just as success of the
Soviet movement in China would have important effects in
India and Japan, so too would a Communist revolution in
Germany, or a Fascist coup in Japan, have tremendous
effects on the Asia continent.

A social revolution, such as China is now going
through, is frustrated unless it has its roots in the
great body of the people. The development that suffered
a break in 1927 has now, five years later, evidently
reached another nodule in the progression from an
Imperial federalism to democratic institutions more
consonant with the times. The development will apparently
be slowly toward a form of State socialism, with the
San Min Chu I and the Kuomintang and its ghostly adviser
all to be dropped. It is to be expected that the actual
pressure of economic circumstance will make requisite an
attitude on the part of the new Chinese nation that will
not be characterized generally by open hostility toward
other countries. But that may not be said certainly.

ANNEX A.   LIST OF RED ARMIES.

ARMY	LEADER	LOCUS	STRENGTH
1:	Hsü Chi-sheng (許 継 慎)	s.e.Honan	15,000
2:	Ho Lung (賀 龍) (Tuan Teh-ch'ang (段 徳 昌), lieutenant)	Hupeh	15,000
3:	Huang Kung-lueh (黄 公 畧)	s.Kiangsi	6,000
4:	Lin Piao (林 彪)	w.Fukien	6,000
5:	P'eng Teh-huai (彭 徳 懐)	s.Kiangsi	10,000
6:	K'uang Chi-hsun (鄺 継 勛)	e.Hupeh	10,000
7:	Li Ming-jui (李 明 瑞)	s.Kiangsi- Hunan border	5,000
8:	Li Chien (李 傑) (formerly,Hsiang Ying (項 英))	s.Kiangsi	6,000
9:	Ts'ai Sheng-chi (蔡 盛 基)	s.e.Honan	2,000
10:	Chou Chien-p'ing (周 建 屏) (controls Fang-Shao duo)	n.e.Kiangsi	5,000
11:	Li Ming-kuang ( )	e.Kuangtung	1,000?
12:	Lo Ping-hui (羅 炳 輝)	w.Fukien	6,000
13:	Hu Kung-mien (胡 公 冕)	Chekiang	5,000
14:	Li Ch'ao (李 超)	Kiangsu- Anhui border	1,500
15:	Ch'en Tzu-p'ing (陳 資 平)	s.e.Honan	5,000
16:	K'ung Ho-ch'ung (孔 荷 寵)	Hupeh-Kiangsi border	10,000
17:	?	Poseh region? (Kuangsi)	3,000?

ARMY	LEADER	LOCUS	STRENG
18:	Hsiao Fang? (肅　芳)	w.Anhui?	10,00
19:	?	Hopei?	1,00
20:	Liu T'ieh-ch'ao (劉 鉄 超)	s.Kiangsi	1,50
21:	Chang Ting-ch'eng (張 鼎 丞)	Kiangsi	1,50
22:	Ch'en I (陳　毅)	s.Kiangsi	5,00
23:	Chang Hsiang-shan? (張 香 山)	n.Hupeh?	5,00
24:	Ho Kuang? (赤阝 光)	Suiyuan- Shensi	2,50
25:	Lo Kuei-po (羅 桂 波)	s.e.Kiangsi	1,00
26:	Yang Yueh-pin (楊 岳 斌)	s.e.Kiangsi	1,00
			140,00

*This total does not include Red Guards, Youth Vanguards,
Young Pioneers, or other similar volunteer organizations.
The strength of these cannot be computed with any
exactitude, because the designations may signify in one
case a group of peasants armed with clubs and in another
a unit of formidable militia; but they doubtless number
many more than the regular Red troops, although with muc
inferior equipment (except perhaps in the case of the
Vanguards).

ANNEX B.   LIST OF REVOLUTIONARIES.

Chang Ch'ang-sheng (張 長 勝), Honan militarist.

Chang Hsiang-shan (   ), Hupeh militarist, in control in the Tsaoyang area. He was reported to have been wiped out in early 1931, but he is evidently still in northern Hupeh. He is the leader of the 23rd Army?

Chang I-yun (張 逸 雲), lieutenant of Li Ming-jui, supposed to be in the Lienhua region. He is a graduate of the Paoting Military Academy.

Chang Kuo-shou (張 國 壽), in the Communist organization at Shanghai. He was reported to have been the successor to Li Li-san as Chairman of the CC of the Party.

Chang T'ao (張 濤), a subordinate of K'ung Ho-ch'ung.

Chang Ting-ch'eng (張 鼎 丞), leader of the 21st Army in Kiangsi.

Chang T'ung-piao (張 同 標), Honan militarist.

Ch'en I (陳 毅), leader of the 22nd Red Army.

Ch'en Shao (陳 韶), militarist in n.w. Kiangsi.

Ch'en Ting-hou (陳 定 侯) divisional commander under Hsu Chi-sheng.

Ch'en Tse-min (   ), leader in CCP at Shanghai.

Ch'en Tu-hsiu (陳 獨 秀), leader of the CCP until 1927. He studied in Japan and France, and was an associate of Hu Shih in the Peking National University, where he headed the Department of Literature. He also edited La Dunesse. He has been expelled from the CCP, and is now probably in Hongkong.

Ch'en Tzu-p'ing (陳 資 平), leader of the 15th Army in s.e. Honan.

Cheng Hung-yi (   ), leader of CCP in Shanghai.

Cheng Hsing-wei (鄭 行 為), until recently the Chairman of the Honan-Anhui-Hupeh Soviet Government; possibly thrown out of power in the turn-over of early 1932.

Ch'eng K'o-ch'un (稈 克 純), rumored to have succeeded Chang Hsiang-shan to control in the Tsaoyang Soviet region.

Ch'i Teh-wei (齊 德 威), divisional commander in s.e. Honan.

Chou Chien-p'ing (周建屏), head of the 10th Army in n.e. Kiangsi.

Chou Chin-ming (周金銘), Tientsin Communist, captured by the police in September 1931; probably executed.

Chou En-lai (   ), Chairman of Organization Committee of CCP, executed in June 1931.

Chou I-li (   ), divisional commander in s.e. Honan.

Chou Wei-chiung (周 維烱), head of the Honan Soviet organization at the time of the capture of Shangcheng, in 1930.

Chu Teh (朱   德), military head of the Soviet Government in Kiangsi. He is said to be a Yunnanese who joined Sun Yat-sen in 1921 with the military forces of his native province. He later went to Germany to study, and on his return became a member of the Communist Party. He was in Nanchang as commander of Hankow Government troops at the time when Ho Lung and Yeh T'ing got control in 1927, and joined up with those leaders in their drive toward the south. He has been one of the outstanding revolutionary figures since that time.

Chu Wei-hsun (朱 讜勳), divisional commander under Chu Teh, reported captured in action in 1931.

Fang Chih-min (方 志 敏), leader of the 10th Army, under the control of Chou Chien-p'ing. He is a graduate of the Nanchang Military Academy (and/or Shanghai College?) who has been to the U.S.S.R. (for study?).

Feng Kung (   ), Left-wing novelist, born 1907. She was executed by the Shanghai authorities in 1931.

Fu Po-ts'ui (傅 相翠), leader in s.w. Fukien. He declared allegiance to Nanking in June 1931, but it is not known what side he is on at present.

Ho Hsiang (何   香), Ho Lung's second sister, in the 2nd Army.

Ho Kuang (郝   光), leader of the section of Kao Kuei-tzu's troops that revolted and "went Red". Probably the present leader of the 24th Army, which is thought to have those revolting troops as its nucleus.

Ho Lung (賀　　龍), head of the Hupeh Red troops and
at the same time leader of the 2nd Army. Ho Lung
was a military commander under Wu P'ei-fu for
several years, in Szechuan. In 1926, he was
stationed on the Kueichow border, at first giving
support to Yeh K'ai-hsing. With the continued
advance of the Canton Reds, however, Ho Lung
changed his allegiance and accepted a place in
T'ang Sheng-chih's 10th Revolutionary Army, being
made commander of the 8th Division. He was closely
associated with the Borodin group in Hankow until
the break-up in 1927, at which time he commanded a
division of Chang Fa-k'uei's Iron Army (20th
Revolutionary Army). With the break-up, he and
Yeh T'ing withdrew to Nanchang, and there declared
their independence of Wuhan on July 30th, in the
name of a Revolutionary Committee purporting to
comprise Madame Sun Yat-sen, Eugene Ch'en, Teng
Yen-ta, T'an P'ing-shan, Su Shao-ch'ing, and others.
Driven from Nanchang by Chang Fa-k'uei, he moved
southwards in a revolutionary career which has
continued without interruption until the present.
He is supposed to be of peasant origin.

Ho Man (賀　　滿), Ho Lung's youngest sister, in the
2nd Army.

Ho Ying (賀　　英) Ho Lung's eldest sister, leading a
unit of the 2nd Army. The general opinion concerning
Ho Ying and her troops, as held by the native press,
is summed up by one writer's characterization of
them as "whores in red leggings" (another paper would
have it "red kerchiefs"), but in the capture of
Huanglingchi by those troops it was discovered that
most of her soldiers are men, and that they all fight.

Hou Yeh-pin(　　　　　), Left-wing poet and novelist,
born in 1905. He was executed by the Shanghai
Gendarmerie Headquarters in 1931.

Hsiang Chung-fa (向　忠　發), the Chairman of the CC of the
Chinese Communist Party from November 1930, when he
replaced Li Li-san. He was a Hupeh man who had
originally started life as a laborer, then became
connected with the CCP after its rise to power. After
1927, he stayed in Moscow for a considerable period
of time, and upon his return earned the cognomen of
"The Stalin of China". He was arrested in the
French Concession /on June 22, 1931, and shot on June
23rd.

Hsiang Ying (項　　英), a leader in the CCP at shanghai.
He formerly controlled the 8th Army.

Hsiao Fang (蕭　　芳), leader of the 18th (?) Army in
w.Anhui.

Hsiao K'o (蕭　　克), Honan militarist.

Hsu Chi-sheng (許 繼 盛), leader of the 1st Army in
(or, shen)   (or 愼), s.e. Honan. He is a
Whampoa cadet.

Hsu Hung (徐　洪), divisional commander under K'ung
Ho-ch'ung.

Hsu Hsiang-ch'ien (徐 象 謙), divisional commander in
s.e. Honan.

Hsu Mu-chien (許 目 兼), divisional commander in
1st Army.

Hu Chu-sheng (胡 竹 笙), Kiangsi militarist.

Hu Kung-mien (胡 公 冕), leader of the 13th Army.

Huang Chih-tao (黃 智 道), Kiangsi militarist.

Huang Kung-lueh (黃 公 略), leader of the 3rd Army.
Huang is a native of Siangtan (Hunan), and a graduate
of the Whampoa Military Academy. He was commander
of a battalion at Pingkiang, where he and P'eng
Teh-huai mutinied because their troops had not been
paid for a considerable period of time, and led the
troops to Chingkangshan to combine with Chu Teh.

Jou Shih (　　　　), teacher and Left-wing essayist and
novelist, born in 1901. He was executed by the
Shanghai Gendarmerie Headquarters in 1931.

Kao Chin-t'ing (高 金 亭), rumored to be the successor
to Chang Hsiang-shan in the control of the n. Hupeh
Soviet area.

Ku Tao-chung (古 道 中), Kiangsi militarist.

K'uang Chi-hsun (鄺 繼 勛), leader of the 6th Army in
e. Hupeh. He is a former Szechuan officer,
serving under Ho Lung in w. Hunan, but later formed
a separate group. He probably did not accompany
Ho Lung south in 1927. He is a graduate of a
military school.

K'ung Ho-ch'ung(孔 荷 寵), leader of the 16th Army.

Kuo Chen-ch'ang(　　　　), leader in CCP in Shanghai.

Li Ch'ao (李　超) leader of the 14th Army.

Li Chieh 李　傑), successor to Hsiang Ying as
commander of the 8th Army in Kiangsi.

Li En-mei (　　　　), leader in CCP in Shanghai.

Li Hen-ping (李 恨 氷), divisional commander under
Ho Lung.

- 119 -

Li Li-san (李 立 三), prominent in the councils of
the CCP in China, possibly at present Chairman
of the Propaganda Committee. He was the son of
a rural school-teacher in Hunan who went to
France during the War to organize the Chinese
coolie labor there. Returning, he became a
prominent labor organizer in the 1926-7 movement,
and after the CCP broke with the Kuomintang he
succeeded to the leadership that Ch'en Tu-hsiu
was forced to relinquish. Li Li-san himself lost
the Chairmanship of the CC in November 1930.

Li Ming-jui (李 明 瑞), leader of the 7th Army, in
s. Kiangsi. He was originally a Kuomintang
general, stationed in s. Hunan. Some time in
1930 (?) he revolted with his troops, which he
first called The Army for Saving the Country
(救 國 軍). Unsuccessful as an independent
unit, he definitely joined up with the Reds, and
now controls the Lienhua area on the Hunan-Kiangsi
border.

Li Ming-kuang (   ), e. Kuangtung militarist,
leader of the 11th Army. He is a graduate of
Whampoa Military Academy.

Li Pu-yun (李 步 雲), Hupeh militarist, formerly in
the s.w. part of the province. When Ho Lung left
that area with his main forces, Li was unable to
hold out against the regulars, and was forced to
relinquish the area. He is now with Ho Lung.

Li Ta-chao (李 大 釗), an associate of Ch'en Tu-hsiu,
executed by Chang Tso-lin.

Li Ts'an (李 燦), commanding the crack troops of
the s.e. Honan Soviet organization.

Li Wei-sen (   ), Left-wing essayist and translator,
born in 1903. Buried alive at Lunghua (near Shanghai)
by the Shanghai Gendarmerie in 1931.

Li Wen-lin (李 文 林), Kiangsi militarist.

Li Yu-chün (李 幼 軍), subordinate of K'ung Ho-ch'ung.

Lin Piao (林 彪), leader of the 4th Army in w. Fukien.

Liu (劉   ), political officer of Ho Lung.

Liu P'ei-jan (劉 沛然), Hupeh militarist in first
independent division.

Liu P'ei-yun (劉 沛 雲), e. Hunan militarist.

Liu Teh-hsin (劉 德 新), Kiangsi militarist.

Liu T'ieh-ch'ao (劉鉄超), Kiangsi militarist.

Liu Wan-ch'un (劉萬春), Kiangsi militarist.

Liu Ying (劉英), leader of 73rd division s.e. Honan.

Lo Kuei-po (羅桂波), leader of the 25th Army, s.e. Kiangsi.

Lo Ping-hui (羅炳輝), leader of the 12th Army in w. Fukien.

Lu Hsiung-yi (   ), member of CCP in Shanghai.

Ma Fu-ming (馬甫明), woman leader of cavalry detachment under Ho Ying.

Mao Chung-ch'u (毛忠初), Honan militarist.

Mao Tse-tung (毛澤東), political officer under Chu Teh, is also one of the chiefs of the soviet organization of Kiangsi. He studied in France.

P'an Teh-wei (彭德瑋), divisional commander in s.e. Honan.

P'eng Teh-huai (彭德懷), leader of the 5th Army in Kiangsi. He was formerly a Colonel in the regular army under Ho Chien, stationed at Pingkiang in 1928. He and Huang Kung-lueh together turned over to the Reds. He is reported to have negotiated with Li Tsung-jen to enter the ranks of Li when the Kuangsi General invaded Hunan in 1930, but the negotiations fell through. He is a native of Siangtan (Hunan), and a graduate of the Paoting Military Academy (having received his intermediate education in a French mission school?).

Shao Shih-p'ing (邵式平), lieutenant of Fang Chih-min who leads the 10th Army in n.e. Kiangsi.

Soong Ch'ing-ling (宋慶齡)- Madame Sun Yat-sen), a native of Kuangtung and a graduate of Wesleyan. She married Dr. Sun in 1916, and was elected a member of the CEC of the Kuomintang in 1926. She is still nominally a member, but she left China in 1927 immediately after the fall of the Hankow Government and has refused to have anything to do with the Kuomintang, or the Nanking Government, since that time. It is probable that she is a member of the "Third Party" group, just as was Teng Yen-ta.

Su Yü-sheng (蘇雨生), leader of a band with undetermined characteristics at Wuyuan, in Suiyuan.

Su I-hung (蘇亦雄), subordinate of Shao Shih-p'ing.

T'an P'ing-shan (譚平山), with Ch'en Tu-hsiu and Li
Ta-chao making up the trio that led the CCP until
the purging of the ranks that followed upon the
fall of the Hankow Government, in which he headed
the peasant-labor block in the CEC. He was
formerly the Canton representative to the Comintern,
but he now is rated as a Menshevist, having fallen
from grace and become a leading figure in the
Third Party. He is a native of Kuangtung, and
graduated from the Peking National University.

T'an Szu-ts'ung (譚思聰), leader of the 1st
Independent Division in Hupeh.

T'ang   (唐   ), militarist in 10th Army in
n.e. Kiangsi.

Teng Yen-ta (鄧演達), a native of Kuangtung and a
graduate of Paoting Military Academy. He became
a Communist in 1924, at which time he was a
member of the staff of the Whampoa Military
Academy. He studied in Germany in 1925, and on
his return in 1926 was made Educational Director
of the Academy by Chiang Kai-shih. He next
succeeded Ch'en Kung-po as Chief of the Political
Training Department, and in March 1927 became a
member of the presidium of the Military Council
and concurrently President of the Wuhan Military
Academy. He left for Moscow after the fall of
the Hankow Government, and became the recognized
leader of the "Third Party" (Left of the Leftist
Kuomintang, but Right of the Communists, and
favoring cooperation with the latter), which has
its headquarters in Berlin. He returned from
Moscow presumably in mid-summer of 1931, and was
arrested by the police in Shanghai about August
15th. Despite the personal appeal of Madame
Sun Yat-sen, Chiang Kai-shih order his execution,
and he was killed a few days later.

Ts'ai Sheng-chi (蔡盛基), Honan militarist.

Ts'ao Hsiao-k'ai (曹効凱), head of Honan Politbureau.

Tseng Cheng-ch'u (曹正初), Kiangsi militarist.

Tseng Ping-ch'un (曹炳春), Kiangsi militarist.

Tseng Ping-shou (曹炳壽), Kiangsi militarist.

Tsung Hui (   ), a student Communist and Left-wing
writer, born in 1910. He was executed by the Nanking
authorities in February 1931.

Tuan Teh-ch'ang (段德昌), formerly a subordinate of
Ho Lung, he was for over a year separated from the
main body of Ho's troops, during which time they
both grew in strength. He is now Ho Lung's chief
lieutenant, commanding about 5,000 men.

Wang Ho-chieh (王 和 儞, Honan militarist.

Wang I-nan (汪 以 南), Honan militarist.

Wang Ping-nan (王 炳 南), Ho Lung leader in w. Hunan.

Wang Ying (王 英), in the Wuyuan (Suiyuan) area.
He at first led an independent body of men in
Suiyuan, later being given regular standing, and
a promise of regular supplies and pay, by Fu Tso-yi
(傅 作 義). In return, Wang was expected to
proceed against Su Yü-sheng and rid the area of
that bandit. Apparently, Fu's promise turned out
to be barren, for Wang Ying was forced to return
to his former standing and live off the country.
He and Su Yü-sheng are now in the same general
district, and the Government proposes to "suppress"
him. In view of the political aspirations of both
Wang and Su, and the fact that there is a Red Army
supposed to be operating somewhat farther east
(taken in conjunction with the fact that there are
Communist seeds planted all along the railway), it
seems possible that either Wang or Su, or both
together, may combine with the 24th Red Army or
otherwise "go Red".

Wei Chin-ch'en (   ), Honan militarist.

Wu Chung-hao (伍 仲 豪), Kiangsi militarist.

Wu Kuang-pao (吳 光 寶), Commissioner in charge of
economic activities in the Honan Soviet region.

Yang Tzu-feng (楊 子 峯), Kiangsi militarist.

Yang Yueh-pin (楊 岳 斌), leader of the 26th Army.

Yeh T'ing (葉 挺), like Ho Lung an officer in
Chang Fa-k'uei's 20th Revolutionary Army in 1927.
He and Ho Lung seized power in Nanchang with the
fall of the Hankow Government, and, after being
driven from that place, Yeh T'ing led the army
that captured Swatow. He and Ho Lung after the
defeat at Canton held power in the Haifeng-Lufeng
region in e. Kuangtung region for six months,
after which time Yeh T'ing was evidently not
heard from again. He is probably dead.

Yin Ch'ao (殷 超), a Ho Lung leader in w. Hunan.

Yin Fu (   ), a student Communist and Left-wing
writer, born in 1909. He wrote children's poems,
and worked among the child workers in Shanghai.
Executed by the Shanghai Gendermerie Headquarters
on February 7, 1931.

ANNEX C. FACSIMILE OF CHINESE SOVIET CURRENCY.

"Kiangsi Bank of Industry & Agriculture" - $1.00

ANNEX D: <u>MAP.</u>

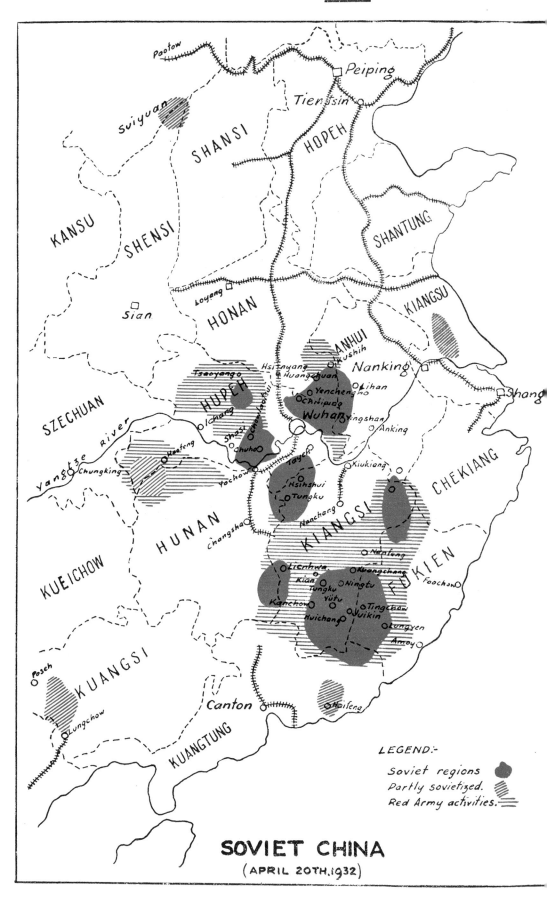

LEGEND:-
Soviet regions
Partly sovietized.
Red Army activities.

SOVIET CHINA
(APRIL 20TH, 1932)